# Arthur Koestler

# Literature and Life Series
(Formerly Modern Literature
and World Dramatists)

Selected list of titles:

Complete list of titles in the series available from publisher on request.

# Arthur Koestler

by

Mark Levene

Frederick Ungar Publishing Co.
New York

**Library of Congress Cataloging in Publication Data**

Levene, Mark.
　　Arthur Koestler.

　　(Literature and life series)
　　1. Koestler, Arthur, 1905-　　—Criticism and inter-
pretation.　I. Title.　II. Series.
PR6021.04Z637　1984　　　　828'.91209　　　　82-40271
ISBN 0-8044-2516-7
ISBN 0-8044-6412-X (pbk.)

*For Kathy, Marissa, and Gillian*

# Contents

# Chronology

| | |
|---|---|
| 5 September 1905 | Born in Budapest, the only child of Henrik and Adela Koestler. |
| 1914-15 | Financially diminished, the family moves to Vienna. His secondary education emphasizes science and modern languages. |
| 1922-26 | Attends a polytechnic in Vienna, where he studies science and becomes an ardent member of a Zionist dueling fraternity and follower of the militant Vladimir Jabotinsky. Destroys his matriculation book and leaves the college. |
| 1926 | Travels to Palestine as a member of Jabotinsky's Revisionist Party. Does menial jobs in Haifa. |
| 1927-30 | Becomes Middle Eastern correspondent for the German Ullstein newspapers. Moves to the Ullstein News Service in Paris. |
| 1930 | Early success in appointments as science editor of the *Vossische Zeitung* (Berlin) and foreign editor of the *Berliner Zeitung am Mittag*. |

| | |
|---|---|
| 1931 | The only journalist on the Graf Zeppelin Arctic Expedition. |
| 31 December 1931 | Joins the German Communist Party. |
| 1932-33 | Dismissed by Ullsteins because of clandestine work for the Communist Party. Travels to Russia to write about the Five Year Plan. Drafts a play in Moscow. Visits Budapest. |
| 1933-35 | Works intermittently for Willy Muenzenberg's Comintern projects in Paris. Writes an *Encyclopedia of Sexual Knowledge* and begins work on *The Gladiators*. Marries Dorothy Asher (separated 1937, divorced 1950). |
| 1936-37 | Makes three trips to Spain after outbreak of the Civil War. Party propagandist and correspondent for the London *News Chronicle*. Captured by Franco's Nationalists at Malaga and sentenced to death. Imprisoned in Seville. Freed after British protests. Publishes *Spanish Testament*. |
| 1938 | Travels to Paris, Athens, and Palestine for the *News Chronicle*. In Paris resigns from the Communist Party. |
| 1939-40 | His first novel, *The Gladiators*, is published. Writes *Darkness at Noon*. Interned in a French prison camp for aliens. Released because of British |

|  | pressure. Joins the French Foreign Legion and escapes to England. |
|---|---|
| 1941-42 | *Darkness at Noon*, his second novel, is published in the English translation. After serving in the British Pioneer Corps, works for the Ministry of Information. Revises *Spanish Testament* into *Dialogue with Death*. Publishes *Scum of the Earth*, an account of his prison experiences in France. |
| 1943 | *Arrival and Departure*, his first novel written in English, is published. |
| 1944-45 | Commits himself again to Zionism. Publishes his first collection of essays, *The Yogi and the Commissar*. Correspondent for the *London Times* in Palestine. |
| 1946-47 | *Darkness at Noon* is published in France as *Le Zéro et l'Infini*, eliciting intense political controversy. Works with Orwell toward forming a new League for the Rights of Man. *Thieves in the Night*, his pro-Zionist, anti-Jewish novel, is published. Visits Paris for the production of his play, *Bar du Soleil*. Personal and ideological tensions with de Beauvoir and Sartre. Writes *Insight and Outlook*, the first version of his theory of creativity. |

| | |
|---|---|
| 1948-49 | Travels to the United States for a literary and Cold War publicity tour. Lectures at Carnegie Hall. With the end of the British Mandate, decides to visit Palestine as correspondent of English, American, and French newspapers. Publishes *Insight and Outlook* to uncertain reactions. Publishes *Promise and Fulfilment*, his study of Palestine and Zionism. |
| 1950 | Publishes with others his anti-Communist memoir, *The God That Failed*. Marries Mamaine Paget. Works toward the formation of the Congress for Cultural Freedom in Berlin. Delivers major speech to the Congress. Virulent Stalinist responses to his participation. Visits the United States. Efforts made to secure him the right of permanent residence. Buys Island Farm on the Delaware River. |
| 1951-52 | *The Age of Longing*, his fifth novel, is published. Alters plans to live in America. Publishes *Arrow in the Blue*, the first volume of autobiography. |
| 1953-54 | Abandons draft of a new novel. Divorced from Mamaine, whose sudden death occurs in June 1954. Publishes *The Invisible Writing*, the second volume of autobiography. |

| | |
|---|---|
| 1955 | Publishes collection of essays, *The Trail of the Dinosaur*, his valedictory to political writing and ideological controversy. |
| 1956 | Involvement with the movement against capital punishment. Publishes *Reflections on Hanging* to considerable effect. Begins work on his history of scientific creativity. |
| 1957 | Becomes a Fellow of the Royal Society of Literature. |
| 1959-61 | Publishes *The Sleepwalkers*. Travels to India and Japan to survey Eastern ethics. Publishes *The Lotus and the Robot*. Establishes a prize for artistic work by prisoners. Lectures on psychology at American universities. Writes second part of trilogy on the life sciences. |
| 1964-65 | Publishes *The Act of Creation*. Visits Stanford University as a Fellow at the Center for Advanced Study in the Behavioral Sciences. Marries Cynthia Jefferies, his secretary since 1950. |
| 1967-69 | Publishes final part of trilogy, *The Ghost in the Machine*. Receives the Sonning Prize from Copenhagen University and an honorary Doctorate of Law from Queen's University. Organizes the Alpbach Symposium on contemporary science and psychology. Publishes |

|  | *Beyond Reductionism*, with J. R. Smythies. |
| --- | --- |
| 1971-74 | Proliferating work in biology and parapsychology. Publishes *The Case of the Midwife Toad* (1971), *The Roots of Coincidence* (1972), *The Call-Girls* (1972), a portrayal of scientific and cultural disputes in novel form, and *The Challenge of Chance*, with Sir Alister Hardy and Robert Harvie (1973). Receives further distinctions, a CBE (Commander of the Order of the British Empire) in 1972 and C. Lit. (Companion of Literature of the Royal Society of Literature) in 1974. Publishes volume of essays, *The Heel of Achilles*. |
| 1976-80 | Publishes *The Thirteenth Tribe*, his first reappraisal since the late 1940s of the historical meaning of Jewishness. Publishes two recapitulations of his career, *Janus: A Summing Up* and the omnibus, *Bricks to Babel*. |
| 3 March 1983 | Commits suicide with his wife, Cynthia, in their London home. A note, dated June 1982, explains that the process of Parkinson's Disease and a form of leukemia was becoming acute, demanding that he "seek self-deliverance." His estate to endow a chair in parapsychol- |

ogy at a university in the United Kingdom.

1984        Incomplete third volume of autobiography, *The Stranger on the Square*, written with Cynthia Koestler, is published.

# 1

## The Koestler Life: An Arrow in the Twentieth Century

Until 1940, Arthur Koestler insisted, his life was "the typical case-history of a Central-European member of the intelligentsia in the totalitarian age."[1] Indeed, many intellectuals faced death from Hitler or from Stalin, spent as much time in prisons as in libraries, and never quite recovered from finding a monster in the cradle of the revolutionary paradise. To this extent, Koestler was "typical." But the body of work and the influence that emerged from these years were extraordinary. Even his death and the memories it evoked were remarkable. Few writers have affected men's thinking about politics so immediately and profoundly. Few have matched his fierce sense of commitment to the public world. After Koestler's suicide, David Astor, the former editor of the London *Observer*, said: "He was great in intellect and imagination, and great in moral courage. . . . Koestler will hold a place in the front rank of . . . those who have saved our century from disgrace."[2]

For fifty years Koestler relentlessly pursued an understanding of the human condition. He changed languages, left political writing for scientific discourse, and despite acute frustrations and a profound pessimism, continued to believe that his perceptions could help mankind recognize its great splendors of creativity and its more prevalent diseases. Of his contemporaries only Koestler stayed in the fight for the world's possible

1

redemption. Malraux withdrew into personal style and the patronage of de Gaulle; Silone returned to an unmilitant piety; and before we could easily spare him, Orwell succumbed to the disease that had plagued his last years.

Of these figures, Koestler was perhaps not the greatest writer—in the 1940s his willfulness, zeal, and anger became too imperious—but he left the most commanding of this century's political novels. The inevitable comparison is with Orwell's legacy. For all the fear Orwell continues to inspire, it is still possible to defend one's feelings and intellect against the vision of totalitarianism in *Nineteen Eighty-Four*, of a boot stamping a face forever. It is impossible, however, to resist the blindness and the sorrow of Rubashov, the old Bolshevik in Koestler's *Darkness at Noon*. To borrow the language of another exile though a very different kind of writer, in *Darkness at Noon* Koestler wrote "a chapter of the moral history of his country." But Koestler was not an exile in Joyce's mold. He was a Hungarian who lived in Germany, France, then England; he was a Jew who believed in a complex, lacerating form of assimilation. Koestler's "country," then, was the modern age itself, its umbilicus stretching during the 1930s from the meeting halls of Europe and America, from the mines of Asturias, to Moscow and the Winter Palace. For thousands around the world, Koestler helped cut the cord of revolutionary belief and utopian innocence, a surgery that was not always welcome, and for which he was not always forgiven.[3]

In part because of his years as a Communist, Koestler was a skillful organizer and meticulous researcher. The ultimate form this took was the methodical, exact design of his death and, one assumes, the death of his wife.[4] Thirty years earlier he researched the time of his birth with equal thoroughness. On September 5, 1905, an early phase of the Russian Revolution was underway in Baku. "The events in Baku on my birthday were the prelude to the first general strike in modern history." Somewhat later both Freud and Einstein published major papers. "I was born," he concludes, "at the moment when the sun was setting on the Age of Reason." But whatever blows the Enlightenment was taking under the surface of life, all Koestler's parents, Henrik and Adela, were aware of in Budapest was that the labor had been extremely difficult and that their only child was very large.

Koestler's father had been "an infant prodigy" (together with bankruptcy an endemic trait in the family) and was, throughout Koestler's early years, an unreliable adult. Although his textile business prospered for long periods, finances were often absorbed by grandiose schemes and inventions, such as radioactive soap and an envelope-cutting machine, "the only outlets he found for his explosive imagination." Koestler's mother, on the other hand, was nervous and mercurial. As a girl living in Vienna she suffered from "violent headaches" that briefly brought her to the study and attention of Dr. Freud in about 1899. She told her son that she had disliked Freud intensely: "He massaged my neck and asked me silly questions." Later, she had to move to Budapest to live with a sister and never really accepted the transition.

> She never ceased to regard the Magyars as a nation of barbarians, and though she lived for nearly half a century in Budapest, refused to learn Hungarian properly. This proved to be a blessing where my own future was concerned, for I was brought up bilingually, talking Hungarian at school and German at home. . . . Her contempt for the Hungarians made her life a kind of exile, without friends or social contacts; in consequence, I grew up without playmates. I was an only

child and a lonely child; precocious, neurotic, admired for my brains and detested for my character by teachers and schoolfellows alike.

His sense of loneliness was intensified by his mother's haphazard, "abrupt changes of mood, from effusive tenderness to violent outbursts of temper"—a pattern Koestler himself was to follow in many of his relationships.

Guilt and fear also grew to dominate his childhood. Through a parlormaid, Koestler came to feel that "one acquired guilt automatically, in the same way one's hands grew dirty as the day wore on." But where guilt was a coherent, if menacing, visitation giving shape to the day, fear was sudden and shattering. In 1910 an unexpected, unexplained tonsillectomy performed without anesthesia produced his first trauma: those moments "of choking and vomiting blood . . . of utter loneliness, abandoned by my parents, in the clutches of a hostile and malign power, filled me with a kind of cosmic terror. . . . It is not unlikely that my subsequent preoccupation with physical violence, terror, and torture derives partly from this experience, and that Dr. Neubauer paved the way for my becoming a chronicler of the more repulsive aspects of our time."

During 1914 and 1915 Koestler's precarious sense of stability and permanence was threatened by a painful, "lurid" succession of conflicts between his parents and by the family's relocation to Vienna and a series of boardinghouses. His father's business had disintegrated with the outbreak of the First World War. But Koestler continued with the same kind of education he had been receiving in Budapest; satisfying his interests in physics and engineering, he attended a *Realschule*, which emphasized scientific training and modern languages. His heroes were Darwin, Kepler, Newton, and Marconi, "the Buffalo Bills of the frontiers of discovery." He was skilled at languages, passionate about chess, and deeply perplexed by the unsolvable "riddle" of infinity—that if you shot an "arrow into the blue . . . there would be nothing to stop it, no limit and no end, in space or in time." One of the central perceptions of Koestler's autobiography is that all his utopian obsessions had the same root:

My obsession with the arrow was merely the first phase of the quest. When it proved sterile, the Infinite as a target was replaced by Utopias of one kind or another. It was the same quest and the same all-or-nothing mentality which drove me to the Promised Land and into the Communist Party. In other ages aspirations of this kind found their natural fulfilment in God. Since the end of the eighteenth century the place of God has been vacant in our civilisation; but during the ensuing century and a half so many exciting things were happening that people were not aware of it. Now, however, after the shattering catastrophes which have brought the Age of Reason and Progress to a close, the void has made itself felt. The epoch in which I grew up was an age of disillusions and an age of longing.

At this time the "arrow in the blue" was not Koestler's only preoccupation. He was also troubled by his abbreviated height, by his "preposterously juvenile appearance," and by his uncontrollable shyness and insecurity. But in 1922 the painfulness of adolescence was absorbed by his almost accidental membership in one of the Zionist dueling fraternities at a polytechnic college in Vienna. "Their aim was to show the world that Jews could hold their own in duelling, bawling, drinking, and singing just like other people." Their opponents were Pan-Germanist fraternities that "had adopted a racist doctrine long before the name of Hitler was known." Koestler's three years in this ritualized *camaraderie* remained one of the few thoroughly happy periods in his life. And it was through the Zionist fraternity that his first major political commitment took shape. (He had had an earlier enthusiasm for Béla Kún's short-lived Hungarian commune of 1919.)

When he initially joined the Zionist movement, Koestler knew nothing about Zionism and little about Jews. Although his mother came from an intellectually distinguished Jewish family in Prague, he was "brought up in an assimilated environment without roots in Judaic tradition." But through the Zionist movement in Vienna, Koestler became aware of Yiddish culture and for the first time met Polish and Russian Jews. His reactions were profound and were to stay with him throughout his life. He quickly developed an intense distaste for what he saw as the servility, muddy mysticism, and staleness of the ghetto. He despised the "dishonesty" of Judaism and the physical characteristics of Eastern European, "tradition-bound" Jews—their furtive and cunning looks, their "overripeness." Equally repugnant, lilting sing-song that turned every factual statement into an emotional one. . . . It had no fixed grammar and syntax, no fixed vocabulary, no logical precision." For Koestler Zionism came to mean the potential antithesis of Judaism and the inbred ghetto. A Jewish state, a sense of secure belonging, "seemed a kind of miracle cure for a sick race." In 1924 he became a follower of Vladimir Jabotinsky, a cosmopolitan Zionist from Odessa who was himself "a stranger to Jewish tradition." Jabotinsky's "Revisionists" argued for massive immigration and a Jewish majority in Palestine, for a national army, and "Latinisation of the obsolete Hebrew alphabet."[5]

In the time he had free from Zionist politics, Koestler nurtured the contemplative side of his temperament; he discovered Freud, the "schismatic schools of Adler, Steckel and Jung . . . experimental psychology and the psychology of art." The excitement of all these pursuits crowded out his conventional studies, and in 1925 while his parents were in England trying to resurrect their business, Koestler burned his matriculation book, which effectively destroyed his record of existence at the polytechnic. It was "a literal burning of my bridges, and the end of my prospective career as a respectable citizen and member of the engineering profession." The act was not the expression of an apprentice-artist defining himself in anger and rebellion. He was suddenly and simply enamored "with unreason itself." His sense of irrational exultation passed into remorse for the cost of his education and the betrayal of his parents, but he soon located a purpose for his decision—by putting his theoretical Zionism into practice. With an immigration certificate issued by Jabotinsky's Revisionist Party, Koestler left for Palestine on April 1, 1926.

His destination was the Heftsebā kibbutz in the Valley of Yesreel, the settlement that was "deepest in purely Arab territory." But Koestler failed his probationary period there—his support for Jabotinsky and his lack of agrarian commitment were the main factors—and he "entered upon a period of poverty and semi-starvation, which lasted for about a year." He sold lemonade in Haifa, worked for a tourist agency in Tel Aviv, and left Palestine briefly to run the Revisionist Party's Secretariat in Berlin. Through the intervention of a friend and some impressive bluffing on his part (Koestler had few articles to his credit at this time), in 1927 he began his journalistic career near the top, as Middle East correspondent for the prestigious and liberal House of Ullstein. Vast in the scope of its publications, it was "the embodiment of everything progressive and cosmopolitan in the Weimar Republic." At twenty-two, Koestler felt he was part of the "aristocracy" of European journalism. What he did not realize at the time was that he was being given the opportunity to witness the collapse of European liberalism from within one of its bastions.

He produced a succession of *feuilletons* ("a perverse blend of travelogue, essay and short story") as well as detailed political essays. He traveled extensively in the Middle East, interviewed King Feisel of Iraq, and invented the Hebrew crossword puzzle, "a tricky business because the Hebrew alphabet consists of consonants only." But by 1929 Koestler was tired of Palestine: "Instead of Utopia, I had found reality." He was increasingly repelled by the revival of Hebrew as the everyday language of the community, and Zionism itself was beginning to seem a spent or a paralyzed force. To remain in Palestine would be cultural suicide. "My mind and spirit were longing for Europe, thirsting for Europe." This was the first of many conflicts Koestler experienced between his queasy sense of himself as a Jew and the very definite meanings, the inherent purity, he found in European culture. That the conflict kept repeating itself, that he found different, sometimes byzantine, ways of resolving it, but invariably in favor of European tradition, is a measure of how raw the issue remained for him.

In 1929 Koestler's love-hate relationship with the French began. After a leave in Berlin, he was posted by the Ullsteins to Paris and arrived there on Bastille Day. The city exerted its customary appeal, but Koestler "never saw Paris through the eyes of the tourist." The demands of work forced him to share "from the outset the routine of a French officeworker of average modest income," and as a result he quickly became familiar with the motto of this class: "one must defend oneself." In subsequent years Koestler was again to recognize this defensiveness and smugness in the ambivalence of the French bureaucracy toward war with Germany and in the postwar political logic of the Parisian intelligentsia. Initially, however, it was an oddly attractive attitude to Koestler because it contrasted so sharply with his own sense of adventure and rootlessness.

But Koestler's life in Paris as "paragon of *petit bourgeois* virtue" was brief. Because of his ability to write clearly and simply about complex scientific theories—a skill he virtually perfected over half a century—he was transferred to Berlin in 1930 as "Science editor of Germany's most respected newspaper, and Science adviser to the huge Ullstein trust." Within a year Koestler also became foreign editor of another of the newspapers. Despite all the marks of success, however, he still felt "unbalanced, naive, unsure" of himself. The camouflage of arrogance and aggressiveness he tried on "did not fit, and it produced a jarring tone which set people's teeth on edge." The only relief from his sense of being a fraud, from the feeling of intellectual stagnation, and from his demonic pace of work was the tireless pursuit of women. "The involvements of those years were so many and so intense that they deadened the creative urge. The calories I spent on them would have sufficed for writing half a dozen novels. But they would have been bad novels, and they made good living."

The "phantom chase" after the perfect "Helena" was soon mirrored by Koestler's most lasting attack of "absolutitis"; his gradual conversion to the Communist Party. Koestler had returned to Berlin on September 14, 1930, the day the Nazis increased their vote by 800 percent and went from 12 seats to 107 in the Parliament. To his horror, the Ullstein papers, although belonging to Jews, began to show the effects of the election. Editorials against the Western powers "became stuffy, patriotic and provincial"; the Ullsteins' campaign against capital punishment was abandoned, and oblique efforts to "Aryanize" the firm were made. For Koestler, as for countless intellectuals at the time, the liberal middle class "had betrayed its convictions and dishonoured itself." But the German Socialist Party provided no genuine alternative. While working in Paris, Koestler had developed a strong contempt for its "staleness and apathy." In the early 1930s its record became even more dismal and compromised. By contrast, the Communists seemed not only honorable but also the only vital and determined opposition to Hitler's Fascism.

Koestler threw himself into the study of Communist literature and discovered the personal assurance created by a "closed system" of absolute belief and the comfort of a ritualized hierarchy. "Even the member on the lowest level . . . feels that he is the bearer of [an apostolic authority] whose flame has been passed down to him from the Holy of Holies." Like other converts, Koestler was deeply affected by a "guru" who served as "master and example" to his faith. Koestler was, in his own terms, an "enthusiast," but not a fanatic, a rebel not a revolutionary. The difference for Koestler is that "the former is capable of changing causes, the latter not. . . . The rebel always has a touch of the quixotic; the revolutionary is a bureaucrat of Utopia." To be in love with the Five Year Plan, with the creation of paradise in Soviet steel and concrete, was "an honorable error," a "sincere and spontaneous expression of an optimism born of despair." Inevitably, he had only contempt for those "who derided the Russian Revolution from the beginning." Their reasons "were less honourable than our error."

Curiously, one of the most compelling parts of Koestler's *Arrow in the Blue* is not this analysis of faith and conversion—there is too much that is defensive and self-congratulatory in it—but rather the account of what became the climax of his "career as a journalist": the remarkable flight of the Zeppelin Arctic Expedition in which Koestler participated as the only member of the press. Initially, he thought he might be able to "establish a colony of the future Jewish state in the Arctic," by dropping a number of weighted Zionist flags on to an uncharted island. The Ullstein board turned down the idea as politically inflammatory: "I wish that conference had been recorded; rarely can earnest Prussian executives have grappled with a more surrealistic proposal." He had to be content with the beauty of the Zeppelin itself, with the bizarre conflicts between the Germans and Russians on board, and with the awesomeness of the Arctic: "Around the Cape there was a stretch of open sea, and the colour of the water was black. . . . As we came nearer, the island, glaciers, and rock constantly changed their colour, from red to violet to molten gold, and the sea from black to faint lavender." Because of these scenes, and more generally because of Koestler's ability to create a vivid tone, a strikingly visual aspect of a situation, one can only echo the regret voiced by Bernard Crick that so little of Koestler's "vast journalistic output" remains.[6] In 1940 the French police confiscated his file of newspaper articles, and afterwards Koestler did not see fit to issue even a selection from this early work.

The expedition seemed to make any further success as a journalist unnecessary, and on December 31, 1931, Koestler applied for formal membership in the German Communist Party. He was persuaded, however, to give up his proletarian impulses and to remain in his influential position with Ullsteins where he could pass on information to the Party. In 1932 this arrangement was discovered, and Koestler was quietly dismissed from his job. He moved to the Red Block area of Berlin, where he "was at last permitted to lead the full life of a regular Party member." He distributed pamphlets, canvassed for elections, and shadowed Nazi cars. Although he relished the companionship of his group, the Party's contempt for intellectuals only aggravated his habitual sense of inferiority and guilt. He completely turned against his education, his upbringing, his "powers of reasoning and capacity for enjoyment." But because he still enjoyed "a certain reputation as a liberal journalist," he was given a visa to visit Russia. The cost of the visit to Koestler was to be a series of articles on the Five Year Plan he would write from an ostensibly disinterested, bourgeois perspective.

In 1932 and 1933, at the height of the famine, Koestler traveled through the Ukraine and Soviet Central Asia, from Baku to the Afghan frontier and Tashkent, but the ravages of malnutrition, the epidemics, and the dying villages could not at the time affect his political certainty. "Women were lifting up their infants to the compartment windows—infants pitiful and terrifying with limbs like sticks, puffed bellies, big cadaverous heads lolling on thin necks." Countless men were suffering from grotesque eye diseases; others found relief from their pain by collapsing and dying in the streets. "I was surprised and bewildered—but the elastic shock-absorbers of my Party training began to operate at once. I had eyes to see, and a mind conditioned to explain away what they saw." His ideological filter was equally effective against the beauty of the landscape and the emblems of Russian history: "I set out for Mount Ararat and the city of Bokhara, not to feast my eyes and delve into the past, but to see how they were doing on the Central Asian cotton production front." All Koestler consciously wanted to witness was the progress of revolutionary industrialism. In Moscow and Kharkov he completed a travel book, *White Nights and Red Days*, but it appeared only in an expurgated German edition; a Russian version was not forthcoming because Koestler's style was "too frivolous and lighthearted."

The scenes of suffering and misery he encountered throughout his journey eventually played a part in his break from the Communist Party, but Koestler had two specific experiences in Russia that came to have even more lasting effects on his emotional and artistic life. In Moscow at the end of his travels he "met a number of men in the higher Comintern and Soviet hierarchy, among them Mikhael Kolzov, Karl Radek and Nicolai Bukharin." He had never before seen such exhaustion; these Bolshevik intellectuals and politicians had been worn out by the years of conspiracy and exile, by the Civil War and by the demands of revolutionary power. Of all of them, Radek and Bukharin had a profound but indefinable effect on him. Within a decade they were executed by Stalin, but transformed by Koestler's memory and imagination into Nikolai Rubashov, the Party's ritual offering in *Darkness at Noon.*

A more lacerating experience for Koestler was his betrayal of a lover he calls Nadeshda Smirnova.[7] He was told by a friend connected with the secret police in Baku that Nadeshda and her aunt were suspected of being foreign agents. Although Koestler found this improbable and in Nadeshda's case, preposterous, he nevertheless informed his police friend that she had taken a telegram from his pocket. The possibility that she was just curious about her lover did not occur to him until after he resumed his travels. None of his letters was answered, and Koestler never discovered whether any action was taken against her.

> During my seven years in the Communist Party, the only person whom I denounced or betrayed was Nadeshda, and she was the person dearer to me than anybody during those seven years. It is no exaggeration when I say that I would have died for her readily and with a glow of joy. The Party to which I betrayed her I did not love; I had qualms and doubts about it. . . . But I was part of it, as my hands and my guts were part of myself. It was not a relationship; it was an identity.

Ultimately, the episode made Koestler into "a bad Communist and a bad anti-Communist, and thereby a little more human." It also sharply inhibited his creation of female characters. Over the years Koestler repeated that women are the most poorly portrayed figures in his novels. "The reason is that I like dining with women, talking, listening and making love to women—but to write about them bores me." But he was not "bored" writing about Nadeshda directly out of this terrible experience. In her stateliness, mystery, and fear, she remains the only credible woman in all of Koestler's writing. Perhaps this uniqueness was the one way he could pay his debt to her.

To his relief the Party decided that he should not remain in Russia. "I was a Communist but I found life in Russia terribly depressing." Koestler was delighted to return to Europe, but discovered intimations of doom everywhere as the shadow of Nazism spread. In Vienna the mood was expectant and gray. The students Koestler had once enjoyed had now become "burly louts in leather shorts and white knitted knee-stockings." He went on to Budapest where two Soviet agents had recently been hanged. But Koestler's stay in the city turned out to be almost exclusively literary. The play he had drafted while still in Moscow, *Bar du Soleil*, almost made it into production, and he renewed his friendship with the writer, Andor Németh. Koestler's reprieve from politics was very temporary, however. "My years in Russia had made Utopia recede; but when my faith had begun to falter, Hitler gave it a new, immensely powerful impulse. Thus started my second honeymoon with the Party." In the autumn of 1933 he traveled to Paris and immediately began working for Willy Muenzenberg, the "genius" behind the Party's anti-Fascist campaign in Europe.

After the publication of the *Brown Book*—a consummate work of propaganda that accused the Nazis of responsibility for burning the German parliament—Koestler was assigned to work in the Free German Library. The job itself was congenial, but he was uncomfortable about becoming "a salaried employee.... I wanted to live for the Party, not off the Party; I

wanted to be an amateur Communist, not a professional." Early in 1934 Koestler resigned from the
archive and in order to survive financially he agreed to a
cousin's suggestion that he write a sex book. Koestler
became Dr. Costler and quickly produced *The Ency-
clopedia of Sexual Knowledge*. He also completed a
novel about German refugee children that was rejected
by a Party committee for its "bourgeois, individualistic
tendencies." The Party had now turned down two of his
books, and Koestler's sense of self-pity was boundless.
He even flirted with gassing himself to death, but
pathos became comedy when a book fell off the shelf
and almost broke his nose. In part because of what he
saw as the shabbiness of these "antics," Koestler was
soon working enthusiastically and without pay for a
semischolarly Communist institute set up to study the
nature of Fascist governments.

Within a year, however, the Party bureaucracy
closed down the institute; it was "an altogether too
unorthodox and independent enterprise." To appease
his revived uncertainty about the Party and the course
of the Revolution, Koestler began work on a novel
about the legendary pre-Christian revolt led by the
gladiator Spartacus. During 1935 and 1936 he edited a
comic weekly for Muenzenberg and moved restlessly
between Paris, Budapest, and Zurich, where he married
Dorothy Asher—they parted amicably after a few
months—and met the Italian political novelist Ignazio
Silone, whom he found "wrapped up in . . . a soft but
impenetrable cloud of melancholy and depression."
During this time Koestler wrote a stream of articles and
reviews, half a satirical novel, and again as Dr. Costler,
*Sexual Anomalies and Perversions*. And in the background, after the assassination of Sergei Kirov, Stalin's
purge of the old Bolsheviks began, with the trial and
execution of Zinoviev and Kamenev.

But when the Spanish Civil War broke out in 1936,

Koestler's ties with the Party solidified once more. Spain was "the first country in which the workers and the progressive middle class had jointly taken up arms to resist a Fascist bid for power." Like many others, some with profound doubts about Stalin's purposes, Koestler believed that only the Party had the will and the organization to lead this resistance, to mount what might be the last defense against Fascism in Europe. Koestler returned to Paris and at Muenzenberg's suggestion received accreditation from the London *News Chronicle* to investigate German and Italian intervention on Franco's side. In Seville he was recognized as a Communist and barely evaded arrest. Yet displaying his remarkable courage and moral adventurousness, Koestler returned to Spain, this time escaping from Madrid with documents that proved Nazi complicity in the preparation of Franco's insurrection. In Paris he wrote *L'Espagne ensanglantée*, an explicit work of propaganda that, however, contains only a portion of the emphasis on Fascist atrocities which Muenzenberg had demanded.

His third and final trip to Spain led to what Koestler describes as a rebirth, a "spiritual transformation." After the fall of Málaga in February 1937, Koestler was arrested as a spy and spent three months in Seville under daily expectation of death. In solitary confinement he began to perceive himself as both a finite and an infinite being. As a boy he had once experienced the self's "dissolution and limitless expansion"; here under the pressure of imprisonment and the splintering of his ideological faith, this "oceanic feeling" eroded his "rational, materialistic way of thinking." This process, together with the kinship he felt for the other prisoners, prompted questions about social ethics that later became the central themes of his fiction. "Perhaps the solution lay in a new form of synthesis between saint and revolutionary, between the active and the contemplative life."

He was freed in a prisoner exchange after his wife's tireless lobbying of British officials who pressed his case with Franco. But it took Koestler much longer to free himself from the guilt of "self-abasement," of wanting to come "to terms with the executioners," when he told a warder, "I *no longer* am a *rojo* (Red)." He meant to say that he "never *was* a *rojo*." "The shame of this episode has haunted me for years, as a companion-ghost to that of Nadeshda's figure on the quay at Baku."

In England, Koestler wrote *Spanish Testament* (1937), which brought him to the attention of George Orwell, and separating again from Dorothy, he left for Palestine as a correspondent for the *News Chronicle*. On route he was interrogated by Party officials in Paris about his conduct in prison, and he interviewed Thomas Mann in Switzerland who, in his "ponderous statements," seemed to be "talking for the record." Koestler also met his parents in Belgrade. "It was the last time I saw my father. . . . He still talked of his 'colossal' and 'grandiose' projects, but now his voice had a pathetic ring, and his eyes often shone with the sad tortoise-wisdom of our race." But his "mother was unchanged— resolute, temperamental, caustic and irritable," the mirror image of her son. The six weeks Koestler then spent in Palestine convinced him that "this small and bitter country" no longer "held out a messianic promise, an inspiration for mankind at large." The frighteningly simple issue was the millions of European Jews who had to be given refuge from Hitler. Koestler's articles forcefully argued that the partition of Palestine was both necessary and workable.

After a lecture tour of England for the Left Book Club, he returned to Paris and in the wake of the Moscow Trial of 1938, where the major defendant was Nikolai Bukharin and everything he represented in revolutionary history, Koestler formally resigned from the Communist Party. This decision "filled me with the wild elation that I had experienced every time that I had burned my bridges." Koestler was breaking from the German Communist Party and from Stalinism, yet he retained a belief in the "progressivism" of the Soviet Union "until the Hitler-Stalin pact destroyed this last shred of the torn illusion." He completed *The Gladiators* in July 1938 and immediately began work on another novel for his English publishers that was to be centered on a Bolshevik intellectual who sacrifices morality to expediency. "Before the break, I had thought of myself as a servant of the Cause, and of writing as a means of serving it. Now I began to regard myself as a professional writer, and writing as a purpose in itself."

Writing *Darkness at Noon* proved to be a characteristically dramatic process. Halfway through its composition, Koestler's finances ran out, and he agreed to write another sex book. In Paris he was arrested as an enemy alien and interned for four months together with numerous other anti-Fascists from Germany and Central Europe. In January 1940 he was released, "but continued to be harassed by the police." During the next few months Koestler "finished the novel in the hours snatched between interrogations and searches of my flat." Most of his files and manuscripts were confiscated, but the novel itself was spared, and the English translation was completed and dispatched to London just days before the fall of France. Koestler was arrested again, but on the strength of some brandy and a moment of inspired acting, he talked his way out of the internment camp, joined the Foreign Legion as a Swiss, Albert Dubert, and eventually made his way to England via Casablanca and Lisbon.

Because he had arrived illegally, Koestler was imprisoned in Pentonville, by far the best of the institutions he had experienced, where he corrected the page proofs of *Darkness at Noon* and appraised the reviews when it was published late in 1941. The reviews were generally favorable, but it was Orwell who recognized in the work an authentic and essential understanding of the totalitarian mentality. "Brilliant as this book is as a novel, and a piece of prison literature, it is probably most valuable as an interpretation of the Moscow 'confessions' by someone with an inner knowledge of totalitarian methods."[8] When Koestler left prison, he was already a new literary presence in English intellectual life. He quickly wrote his first book in English, *Scum of the Earth* (1941), a powerful documentary account of his experiences in France. He served in the Pioneer Corps and came to know a number of writers through Cyril Connolly, the influential editor of the literary journal *Horizon*.

David Astor met Koestler at one of Connolly's parties and vividly recalls Koestler's energy, forcefulness, and intensity: "He was in battle-dress, and his hair was cut short. And he seemed to radiate a heightened liveliness and sense of reality. . . . Koestler was the embodiment of an uncompromised, unafraid, international idealism. This small, passionate man, with his excruciating accent, his self-mockery . . . seemed almost as miraculous an apparition, at a different part of the political spectrum, as Churchill himself.[9] Michael Foot's memory is similar: "I first met him in 1940 and fell immediately a swooning victim to his wit, charm and inordinate capacity for debate and alcohol. . . . He was the most formidable arguer I ever saw in action, and I can still lick the wounds he inflicted on me more than 40 years ago."[10]

In 1942 he worked for the Ministry of Information, "writing propaganda pamphlets, broadcasting in German, scripting radio plays and co-directing documentary films."[11] *Darkness at Noon* became a best-seller in the United States, and in 1943 his *Arrival and Departure* was published. Koestler was rapidly becoming one of the most assured and graceful foreign writers of English in this century. But reactions to the novel itself were at best mixed. Its Freudian interpretations of behavior and its overt skepticism about the war were considered puzzling and a moral affront, particularly by Orwell. At this time Koestler also wrote a number of highly effective polemical essays setting out the opposition between the "yogi" and the "commissar," outlining his intensely social aesthetic, and arguing that the Left had to create "a new fraternity in a new spiritual climate."

In 1942 Koestler's Zionism was revived again with the news of the death camps and the British refusal of the refugee ships arriving in Palestine. He worked strenuously (together with John Strachey) for the Anglo-Palestine Committee, and late in 1944 he traveled to Palestine where he pressed the case for Partition with Menachem Begin, then in hiding as head of the terrorist group *Irgun*. It was a futile effort, and Koestler stayed in Jerusalem to draft a novel about the Jewish settlements that he had planned in 1926. It was a haunted, depressing time for him because of all the hatred, "the poisoned atmosphere of . . . savagry and mourning." When Koestler returned to England, he and Mamaine Paget, whom he had met a year earlier, moved into a farmhouse in Wales, where he intended to complete the novel and begin work on a theory of creativity. Here the curiously symbiotic relationship between Koestler and Orwell broadened, "Orwell's critical insight into the strengths and weaknesses of Koestler's work being matched by the latter's insight into the psychology of his critical ally."[12] Along with Bertrand Russell and Michael Foot, they developed plans for creating a non-Communist League for the Rights of Man.

In 1946 the French translation of *Darkness at Noon*, *Le Zéro et l'Infini*, became the center of debate in

France over the nature of Stalinism and revolutionary communism. Because of this controversy, his play, *Twilight Bar (Bar du Soleil)*, was chosen for production by a prominent director, and Koestler returned to Paris to help with the rehearsals.[13] "I had fled from France penniless, with false papers, spat out by a concentration camp, with a kick for a farewell. I came back at the height of the noise around *Le Zéro et l'Infini*, a bestseller and a lion." But this sense of gratification quickly soured. Besides his concern over the fate of the play, which seemed increasingly dismal, Koestler went from frenetic lunches to drunken dinners and a series of terrible quarrels with Sartre and de Beauvoir, even with Camus. Between 1946 and 1949 Koestler, and sometimes Mamaine, made a number of trips to Paris and spent considerable time with the "mandarin" figures of French culture. But most of what occurred was for years carefully omitted from Koestler's autobiography and essays. Only in one essay, "The Little Flirts of St. Germain-des-Prés," did Sartre obliquely appear—with his "myopic little smile" and "impatience to be raped"—but the piece was eliminated from the uniform edition of Koestler's work.

Koestler tried to impress upon the leftist intelligentsia the impossibility of maintaining an independent position, that France would have to make a categorical choice between American support and Russian dictatorship. He succeeded only in convincing them of his passion, his honesty (and, according to de Beauvoir, his almost overbearing self-importance).[14] Their unrepentant leftism, their reluctance to accept his stark anticommunism, posed a threat not only to Koestler's personal sense of worth but also to what he conceived of as the freedom of Europe. Yet Koestler was by no means alone in these positions. To some extent Camus shared his attitudes, at least toward the Soviet Union, and it was Malraux who persuaded Koestler to support de

Gaulle as the one unifying factor in French society. But
Koestler's entire experience with Sartre and de Beauvoir, who he felt were his real equals, was so hateful, so
defined by failure, that he could not approach it
directly in his writing and for decades had to leave the
impression of himself as a detached but horrified
*observer* of the Parisian intelligentsia. In the last years
of his life, however, Koestler began to alter this picture
indirectly, by making his journals from the period
available to his biographer, Iain Hamilton.

Also in 1946 *Thieves in the Night* was published,
again to a variety of response, this time because of
Koestler's support of Jewish terrorism. In *Partisan
Review*, Clement Greenberg said that "its very interest
as a vivid travel book and as a quick introduction to
Palestine politics and society flows from its oversimpli-
cations."[15] For Raymond Mortimer, however, the novel
was "consistently exciting and absorbing . . . a master-
piece of propaganda."[16] Problematic as these responses
were to him, at this time politics and his sense of himself
as a historical novelist were gradually giving way to
science as the pulse of his intellectual life. In 1947 he
completed *Insight and Outlook*, the first phase in his
exploration of creativity and psychology. He was tempted by the idea of spending part of every year in America, since Europe seemed to be suffering from a death
wish and England under Attlee's Labour government
was a land of "virtue and gloom." In 1948 Koestler
sailed for the United States, where he lunched with the
creator of the CIA. He spoke in a number of cities, and
during a press conference remarked about the inevitable comparisons of his work with that of Malraux and
Silone: "I don't think I'm up to them artistically and
there is no false modesty in what I am saying. Politically
it is something else again. I may be more penetrating on
that level." To confirm this, Koestler gave a major
address at Carnegie Hall in which he called on the

"American liberal to grow up" and accept his world-
wide responsibilities.

Koestler became increasingly eager to write a book
about the newly created state of Israel, as a testament to
the struggle of the Jews and again as a way of reassert-
ing his cultural identity. In the summer of 1948 Koestler
and Mamaine arrived in the nation whose existence he
had passionately worked for through two decades.
They visited the kibbutz that appeared thinly disguised
in *Thieves in the Night*, and Koestler felt "like the mur-
derer revisiting the scene of his crime." He interviewed
Begin, for whom he still had "considerable sympathy,"
and pressed the Ben Gurion government to calm its
hostilities to the politically more extreme *Irgun*.[17]
Koestler's support for Begin, circumspect as it was, did
not endear him to many Israelis who already felt
betrayed by his novel. They were soon to be appalled
and revolted by the conclusion Koestler drew from his
own experience and idiosyncratic understanding of
Judaism—that Jews must "return to the Promised
Land," become Israelis, or relinquish their historical
and ethnic separateness and the religion that embodied
it. Hyam Maccoby says: "The setting-up of Israel, he
felt, let him off the hook. He was now free to be the
Gentile, integrated into European culture, that he
always wanted to be. The view that there was no Jewish
culture, only a racialist, tribal attachment, was too con-
venient to him to be subjected to factual examination."[18]

In 1949 Koestler and Mamaine moved to France,
where he finished *Promise and Fulfilment* and continued to see Sartre and de Beauvoir. But tensions (and
quantities of alcohol) were so great that on one occasion
Koestler threw a glass at Sartre and struck Camus, his
only friend in the group. Soon afterwards, Sartre and de
Beauvoir broke completely with Koestler, ostensibly
because of his belief in Gaullism. "Koestler's crisis of
confidence was soon to be displaced by anxiety about

Mamaine."[19] Her chronic asthma grew worse, and she
was temporarily hospitalized. On publication, both
*Insight and Outlook* and *Promise and Fulfilment*
prompted indifferent or hostile reactions, but despite
this frustration, Koestler was soon working hard on *The
Age of Longing*, a novel about the delusions of the
French cultural elite. His secretary was a twenty-two-
year-old South African, Cynthia Jefferies, who as a girl
had determined to work for a writer.

In 1950 *The God That Failed*, a collection of essays
and memoirs by ex-Communist writers, was published
to considerable praise, particularly for Koestler's section. But in January Orwell died. Koestler's opposite in
temperament, Orwell had been both Koestler's pupil
and teacher in the understanding of totalitarian motives
and power. Koestler's eulogy was that Orwell had been
"incapable of self-love or self-pity. His ruthlessness
toward himself was the key to his personality." For
Koestler this lifelong rebel "against the conditions of
society in general and his own particular predicament...
was the only writer of genius among the *littérateurs* of
social revolt between the two wars. . . . I believe that
future historians of literature will regard Orwell as a
kind of missing link between Kafka and Swift."

In April Koestler and Mamaine were married in
Paris, but after an explosion of his formidable temper—
he was not easily persuaded that he was too drunk to
drive—she spent their wedding night with his secretary
and the English poet Stephen Spender. "K is at present
having one of his 'mad fits,' " she wrote, "and has been
for some time; it is the first one since we were in Palestine. This makes him very unpleasant, and is the reason
why whenever we go to Paris he gets stinking and
behaves abominably." But after another explosion, she
also said: "I greatly believe in K as a writer, and I would
do anything, even leave him, if it were necessary to help
him fulfil what I believe to be his destiny. I should count

myself and my life of little importance in such a case."[20]
This astonishing statement of devotion was repeated in
different forms by all the women who were an intrinsic
part of Koestler's life: by Dorothy who, although separated from him, worked to have him released from
prison in Seville; by Mamaine in her remarkable for-
bearance; and most awesomely by Cynthia Koestler
when years later she chose to end her life with his.

In 1950 Koestler, along with other notable ex-
Communists and American government officials,
planned the Congress for Cultural Freedom to be held
in Berlin. Its purpose was to articulate the ideological
problems facing the West and to formulate ways for
intellectuals to counter Soviet propaganda. Koestler
wrote most of the Congress Manifesto and in a commanding speech declared that "socialism has lost its
claim to represent the internationalist trend of humanity." This was a political "landmark" for him because
for years after his break with the Communist Party, he
retained a belief in a revitalized, independent socialist
movement. Sidney Hook recalls that Koestler skillfully
maneuvered behind the scenes, "showed an unwonted
pragmatic disposition to compromise, and turned the
other cheek to barbs hurled at him by some delegates
who thought his formulations too sharp."[21]

Indeed, at this time Koestler was not known for
compromise or disinterestedness. Always volatile, he
could be abusive toward those he considered enemies,
and he was frequently irritable and rude toward
friends. Great bursts of temper, or periods in which
friends were "frozen out," would be followed by elaborate, gracious apologies. "Imbued with *freudisme*, he
tended to read people like an analyst," Raymond Aron
said.[22] He believed passionately in his ideas, without
always believing in the seriousness with which he was
taking himself and the respect he was being given by
others. His boyhood uncertainties and sense of inferior-

ity were never quite absorbed, smoothed out, by his influence and achievements. But his depressions and his aggressiveness had another source. "To think of him as impatient or intolerant," David Pryce-Jones says, "was to fail to perceive how he was governed by deep and admirable rage against the infamy of the times, which, by the law of probability, he ought not to have survived."[23]

In 1950 Koestler also traveled to the United States. With Arthur Schlesinger and James Burnham, he planned the future of the Congress for Cultural Freedom, and in newspaper articles argued for the creation of an elite "Legion of Liberty" that might lead to an integrated European army, then a United Europe. Koestler publicly took sides over the controversial Alger Hiss trial by insisting that the "repentant sinner," Whittaker Chambers, had "performed a service of great social utility." Koestler attributed the public's disapproval of Chambers to the embarrassment and revulsion that apostasy always causes. From their recently purchased Island Farm on the Delaware River, Koestler and Mamaine sought support for the private congressional bill necessary to give him permanent residency.

In 1951 Mamaine determined to separate from Koestler. This painful dislocation combined with the difficulties he was having with the Americans in obtaining a visa and the failure of a lawsuit over Sidney Kingsley's dramatization of *Darkness at Noon* made Koestler change his mind about living in the United States. He finished *Arrow in the Blue*, the first volume of his autobiography, at Island Farm, and in 1952 moved to Montpelier Square in London where, assisted by Cynthia, he wrote the second volume, *The Invisible Writing*. Caught between the strident Right in McCarthy's America and moral as well as personal confusion in France, Koestler decided that England, which had twice given him sanctuary, was his most agreeable

choice. "He had decided . . . to become an English-
man." But through the years he came to realize that "no
foreigner" could ever succeed in this goal. "This amused
him, delighted him, depressed him, impressed him,"
and he "was deeply content to be a 'rootless cosmopolitan.' "[24]

In the summer of 1954 Mamaine died, and Koestler's
essays written afterwards show the darkness in his life
and in his vision of mankind. "The alarming thing is the
coincidence of a period of unprecedented spiritual
decline with an equally unprecedented increase of
power. The Promethean myth seems to be coming true
with a horrible twist: the giant reaching out to steal the
lightning from the gods is morally insane." In the preface to *The Trail of the Dinosaur*, where this essay
appears, he declared: "'This book . . . is a farewell to
arms. . . . Now the errors are atoned for, the bitter
passion has burnt itself out; Cassandra has gone hoarse,
and is due for a vocational change." Koestler was not
evading the image of a maddened Prometheus; he was
searching for another language in which to describe
him. Yet the immediate change was to another kind of
political passion, one, however, that was humanistic
rather than ideological.

In 1955, partly because of his own prior experience
in awaiting execution, Koestler committed himself fully
to the campaign against capital punishment. Although
he had to put aside his work on a biography of Kepler,
he saw the campaign as integral to his more general
concern with man's creativity and destructiveness.
Besides his organizational efforts for the national abolition committee, Koestler wrote a remarkably vivid
assault on the hanging judiciary as a legitimized extension of medieval savagery. *Reflections on Hanging*
(1956), "a history of the controversy . . . over hanging,
during the previous 150 years," was first serialized in
*The Observer*; its editor, David Astor, recalls: "In this

hardhitting campaign, un-English in its disregard of the traditional immunity from debate of the judges, Koestler had the satisfaction of seeing his serious arguments and his powerful evidence gradually convince most of the Press and most of Parliament. He had won many disputations in his life. This was the only time that he won a major social victory."[25]

In 1956 Koestler and Cynthia moved to Kent where he completed his intellectual transition from politics to the world of science with *The Sleepwalkers*, an encyclopedic study of Kepler, Copernicus, and Galileo, which argues that scientific discovery, like all art, has its sources in irrational belief and intuitional leaps. After the book was finished, Koestler abandoned the draft of a new novel, and in late 1958 traveled to India and Japan "to look at the predicament of the West from a different perspective." The result was *The Lotus and the Robot* (1961), an often funny account of Yoga and Zen which concludes that the East seems "to be spiritually sicker, more estranged from a living faith than the West." In the East, as in Israel, Koestler found moral grounds to reconfirm and renew his pride in remaining a European.

In 1961 Koestler convinced the Home Office that an award should be established, funded by him, for artistic work to be done by prisoners. He spoke at Harvard and the University of Michigan, took part in a symposium on drugs and the mind at the University of California, and visited the Parapsychology Laboratory at Duke where he was impressed by both the experimenters and their techniques in studying telepathy and psychokinesis. As his friends and as parts of his autobiography make clear, Koestler had always been interested in the paranormal. (As a boy, he was "much sought after for table-lifting seances," because so many curious things seemed to happen when he was around.) But "he was reticent about such matters. No doubt, having taken on the scientific establishment single-handedly, he was anxious to avoid the added handicap of being branded an occultist or an irrationalist."[26] It took another decade for Koestler to publish *The Roots of Coincidence* (in 1972), his analysis and defense of parapsychological research. After that, he developed "Project Daedalus," experiments in levitation that were conducted at his house in London.

In 1962 Koestler and Cynthia returned to Alpbach in the Austrian Tyrol where they had had a home built. Koestler's work on the second stage in his exploration of the life sciences was briefly interrupted by his drawing together a variety of essays on the social and economic condition of England for the journal *Encounter*. In 1964 *The Act of Creation* was published. A massive analysis of humor, the function of the imagination, and creativity in nature, it was generally well received in the scientific community, but there were some sharp and self-protective attacks on Koestler's understanding of scientific method and his unapologetic assumptions of expertise. The harshest assault came from the zoologist Sir Peter Medawar, who condemned Koestler for not having an "adequate grasp of the importance of *criticism* in science—above all of self-criticism."[27] Because he respected Medawar and because vituperation was no longer his immediate response to attack, Koestler's rebuttal was measured and made the match a draw.

In 1965 Koestler and Cynthia were married in New York, en route to six months at Stanford University's Center for Advanced Study in the Behavioral Sciences. Koestler had earlier insisted that they not marry, since he had already twice proved his unsuitability for married life, but he changed his mind when it seemed that their living together at the university would not be possible.[28] After their stay in California, academic invitations proliferated, but Koestler returned to England in order to finish his trilogy on the mind. *The Ghost in the Machine*, the bleakest of the series in its despairing view of mankind's future, was published in 1967. In part because of the pharmaceutical solution the work demands from biology, one influential reviewer argued that the "book must be considered not as science, but as theology."[29] The vocabulary had changed since his days as a Zionist and a Communist, but Koestler was still in pursuit of an ultimate answer to the plight of the modern world.

Although he never lost his sense of mission, the zealotry, rage, and indignation that were part of the Koestler legend began to disappear during the 1960s. Harold Harris, his editor at Hutchinson, knew him only in these "mellow years" and found him "an extremely endearing author to work with."[30] Koestler "grew milder," Melvin Lasky recalls, "more controlled and, in part, more serenely indifferent to passing irritations ... even on important personal and professional matters."[31] Like many others, I was grateful for this change in mood and temper. When I first met Koestler in 1967, soon after *The Ghost in the Machine* was published, he was generous with his time, thoroughly welcoming, and graciously ambivalent about literary criticism with his work as its object. Still very much the continental intellectual, scattering ideas, ashes, and gossip as he paced around his study, all he seemed to demand was that I not bore him or probe his personal life too closely.

In 1968 Koestler convened the Alpbach Symposium, which was to deal in an independent and unorthodox way with principles of psychology, evolution, and neurology; the edited proceedings became *Beyond Reductionism* (1969). Laying aside the draft of a new novel, Koestler then wrote *The Case of the Midwife Toad* (1971), a compelling portrait of Paul Kammerer, an "anti-Darwinian" zoologist who killed himself when he was accused of tampering with the results of an experiment. In 1972, after *The Roots of Coincidence*,

Koestler finally published another novel, *The Call-Girls*, a satirical and in some ways intensely personal work.

After covering the Spassky-Fischer chess championship in Iceland for the *Sunday Times*, and after retracing his 1940 escape from the French police and the Gestapo, Koestler wrote *The Thirteenth Tribe* as an oblique way of dealing once again with his Jewishness. Published in 1976, this fascinating exercise maintains that the world's surviving Jews are not of Semitic origin but rather are ancestors of the Khazars, "a people of Turkish stock" in the Caucasus region who in the eighth century accepted Judaism as a state religion. Koestler drew the astonishing conclusions that if this is the case, "the term 'anti-semitism' would become void of meaning," and Jews "*must* abandon the racialist pride which alone has kept them in existence."[32] Koestler's last works, *Janus: A Summing Up* (1978) and the omnibus collection, *Bricks to Babel* (1980), are testaments not to cultural or ethnic choices but to Koestler's entire life as a writer. The latter is structured to reflect the transition in Koestler's writing. He realized that readers still identified him with the political work of the 1940s, but seemed assured that *The Sleepwalkers*, *The Act of Creation*, and *The Ghost in the Machine* were together a major work of scientific synthesis and speculation.

When I last saw Koestler in 1977, it was as though this monumental career had never happened. We stood on the steps of his home. He looked down the tailored English square, and the countless distinctions, the forty years in which he changed languages, mastered new disciplines, and brought people to blows over his ideas—for a moment at least they were nothing beside his sadness and bewilderment at the indifference of time, the inevitability of aging. Shortly afterwards, Parkinson's Disease and leukemia were diagnosed, and the final process of physical deterioration began.

In the note he left, dated June 1982, he said: "I wish my friends to know that I am leaving their company in a peaceful frame of mind, with some timid hopes for a depersonalised after-life beyond due confines of space, time and matter and beyond the limits of our comprehension. This 'oceanic feeling' has often sustained me at difficult moments, and does so now, while I am writing this." His one regret was the pain his suicide would cause his wife, Cynthia. Less than a year later, she decided to die with him. At the age of thirteen, she had lived through the suicide of her father, and since her early twenties, when she came to work for Koestler, her life was rarely distinct from his. Her love and patience existed, in his terms, beyond the "confines of space, time and matter," and sometimes beyond the comprehension of their friends.

When Koestler died, the shock was tremendous, unexpected. People who had discounted his scientific work, who, when they thought of him at all, saw him as an anomalous figure—a believer in an age of metaphysical and literary buffoonery—suddenly recalled the moment when they finished reading *Darkness at Noon*, when their entire sense of politics was "riddled with light." In March 1983 they felt the unique loss that comes only with the passing of an age and an individual in whom it was most sharply lived.

# 2

## Silhouettes of History:
## *The Gladiators*

The composition of Koestler's first published novel, *The Gladiators*, took four years and extended over a period of tremendous intellectual, emotional, and physical crisis, probably the most important in his life. When he began work on it in 1934, Koestler's research into the life of the legendary Spartacus provided him with some desperately needed "occupational therapy," with periods of respite from the reason-denying flux of totalitarian Europe and his own increasingly ambivalent allegiance to the Communist Party. At the *Bibliothèque Nationale* in Paris he read everything he could about Spartacus, the free-born Thracian who led the Gladiators' War against Rome in 73 B.C. To give the historical novel its essential texture, Koestler studied "the conditions of slaves in antiquity, the regulations concerning gladiators' fights, the folklore of Thrace and Gaul, the economy of the Roman state, the topography of Mount Vesuvius, and similar subjects."[1] But the therapeutic value of this exotic research was only temporary. Gradually, a sense of the political complexities of the uprising emerged, and with it a sharpening of his doubts about the theory and the practice of Soviet Communism.

Two aspects of the historical situation called into question fundamental doctrines of Marxism, doctrines that had sustained Koestler even during his potentially disillusioning year in Russia: first, the failure of the

Slave Army—despite its initial successes and its great numbers—to overthrow a diseased and enfeebled Rome, and secondly, the astonishing complacency of the majority of Italian slaves. For Koestler the slaves' refusal to respond to the possibility of liberation, to grasp their obvious strength, seemed to contradict the premise in the *Communist Manifesto* that the oppressed would "take their fate into their own hands."[2] The downfall of Spartacus merged in Koestler's mind with the rise of German fascism and the purge trials in Moscow. He was forced to consider whether the subtleties of mass psychology were more substantial than a strict historical absolutism.

> Up to now, I had been critical of the Soviet leadership and the Comintern bureaucracy, but not of the basic teaching of Communism, which I regarded as historically correct, and as self-evident as the axioms of Euclid. Now, the more engrossed I became in my subject, the more questionable became the very foundations of the doctrine ... I wrote the novel in the excited mood of a voyage of discoveries, where every turn opens a new vista.[3]

*The Gladiators* was eventually completed within months of Koestler's resignation from the Communist Party in 1938.

What Koestler dramatizes in the novel is a simple though profound response to oppression which, he believed, was at the heart of every revolution: the unending hope of mankind for a society governed by justice and goodwill. This hope many be inchoate, largely intuitive, as it was in the pre-Christian era, or it may be objectified, rationally expanded, through a comprehensively structured ideology. "It is," Orwell said in his discussion of the novel, "the dream of a just society which seems to haunt the human imagination ineradicably and in all ages, whether it is called the Kingdom of Heaven or the classless society, or whether it is thought of as a Golden Age which once existed in the past and from which we have degenerated."[4] In this sense, Spartacus, Saint-Just, and Lenin are members of the same revolutionary family.

But in "Book One: Rise" the group of fifty or sixty gladiators who have escaped from the Capuan circus have no real goal except to survive. They are little more than a horde of robbers under the command of two men who had been designated "the main feature" in the arena before the escape: Spartacus, leader of the Thracians, "the man with the fur-skin" whose "musing eyes" and quiet manner appeal to the more humane of the gladiators, and Crixus, leader of the Celts, "a gloomy-looking, heavy man with a seal's head and slow, dangerous movements" who represents the rapacious elements in the army, which has begun to swell with slaves and freemen from around the country. When news is brought that a military force has been sent from Rome to destroy them, Crixus withdraws into himself and says nothing, whereas Spartacus's unostentatious authority begins to assert itself. "By and by, every one directed his words to him." In a leap of imagination he counsels a retreat into the crater of Mount Vesuvius, and from there, after ten days under siege, he leads the Slave Army to a brilliant military victory over Praetor Clodius Glaber's larger and more experienced forces.

Although Spartacus's first concern has been the survival of his people, an instinct for justice, an intimation of a larger purpose, has begun to develop. He exhorts a group of reluctant slaves to grasp the freedom that has been offered them, since he "for one cannot see anything...on this estate that you can call your own and could wish to defend with your lives." He rejects the temptation presented by Crixus to escape to an unburdened, hedonistic life in Alexandria. "They'd never catch us. ... There are heaps of women in Alexandria," Crixus says. "It can't be done," Spartacus replies, "not now." His still vague sense of duty draws him instead to "the man with the bullet-head." In the autobiography Koestler notes how in the course of his research he speculated that "Spartacus chose as his mentor and guide a member of the Judaic sect of Essenes, the only sizeable civilised community that practised primitive Communism at that time."[5] In the novel, the Essene, looking almost "amazed at his own dream," addresses Spartacus as the "liberator of slaves, leader of the disinherited" and recounts prophecies of the coming of "One like the Son of man." Spartacus implicitly accepts the Essene's utopian vision of a free and equal society and takes his place in the "gigantic relay race" in which again and again one man stands up and receives the "Word, and rushes on his way with the great wrath in his bowels." Like Koestler's other heroes, Spartacus has embarked on a messianic quest.

The second part of the novel, "The Law of Detours," details the consequences of this quest and the growth of the myths, the beliefs, surrounding Spartacus. He has become "that adversary born to Rome, that hero of tall stature clothed in only a fur-skin, who received the poor and oppressed into his avenging horde." To deal with the turmoil and factionalism that have accompanied the thousands of new arrivals, Spartacus calls a meeting of representatives of the army. His intention is to emphasize practical issues, such as the need for provisions, shelter, and siege machinery. Instead, as he speaks from within the crater of Vesuvius, his words begin to erupt from an "unknown" part of his being, and he calls on his followers to join in the creation of a "Sun State" where the Many will not serve the Few. "He spoke of the anger of the fettered and oppressed which weighted down heavily over Italy, told them how this wrath had dug roads to roam like the brooks that spring forth from the pressure and sweat of the mountains . . . how necessary it was to dam the flow and guide it, so its force might not be wasted . . . how the brotherhood of Slave Towns would grow up in Italia; the great state of justice and goodwill."

Although many of his followers sense that Spartacus embodies their deepest and most hidden feelings—what he said "was exactly that which scorched your own tongue"—his utopian injunction seems merely to hang in the air, while social divisions within the army solidify. The original gladiators have formed an elite and wear Roman uniforms, and the Celts remain more interested in plunder and vengeance than in primitive socialist ideology. A number of towns are destroyed, and in Capua patriotic speakers easily persuade the serfs to unite with their masters against the Slave Army. Instead of saviors, they have become "a horde of demons," a "baneful curse" on the land. Spartacus "did not know how it had happened, nor how it could have been prevented; all he knew was: it was Crixus's fault." To keep his messianic vision alive, Spartacus engineers the separation of the "two kinds of people" in the army, a tactic that results in the massacre of the "greedy" dissidents by the Romans. He has regretfully decided that man "must tread the evil road for the sake of the good and right." He has purged his enemies (although Crixus himself survives the slaughter), and after another major victory over a Roman force, he is in control of all southern Italy. Now Spartacus's just commonwealth can come into being.

The city itself is built on the "ruins of mythical Sybaris," once part of the Golden Age of justice and compassion. But the words Spartacus absorbed from the Essene seem almost as distant now. The Sun State Koestler pictures in Book Three is shaped by the pressures of political expediency and defined by the emblems of a rigid hierarchy. Spartacus forms an alliance with pirates, and Fulvius, his chief adviser, explains to the Councillors of Thurium, a neighboring city, that they should not feel threatened by the Sun State as long as they continue to provide necessary provisions. Thurium's social structure will remain intact; no effort will be made to win over their slaves, because "security for the new city" takes precedence over fomenting revolution throughout Italy.

A newly arrived slave looks for signs of joy and excitement in the Sun State, but there is no moral passion, no sense of a "great experiment" underway. All he hears are complaints about work and the constant demands for discipline that emanate from the tent which now flies the purple velum of a Roman Imperator. In their anger at Spartacus, many rediscover Crixus. "He decreed no laws and issued no commands, did not negotiate with foreign ambassadors. . . . They felt drawn to him in a different, turbid way to which they could give no name, they saw in him the dismal embodiment of their fate." Their frustration with abstract purposes, their lack of immediate pleasures, explodes in a brutal assault against the town of Metapontum, which Spartacus interprets as a challenge to his power and a threat to the existence of the Sun State. It is within his grasp to have a wholesale purge of all the "apostates," but he finally refuses "the very bloody and very unjust detour which alone could lead to salvation." This decision, Koestler insists, dooms the revolution to failure.

In "Book Four: Decline," Spartacus and his army find themselves cut off from a safe retreat by the trench Marcus Crassus, the Roman leader, has had dug across Italy. To save some of his followers, Spartacus tries to appeal to Crassus's sense of humanity, but he encounters only cynicism and self-interest. When the gladiators break out of the trap, Crassus ruins his hope for political dominance in Rome by demanding that the Senate recall his rival, Pompeius. To console himself for being frightened by the specter of Spartacus's power, Crassus crucifies the remaining "insurgents" in two rows along the Appian Way leading to Rome. As the Roman soldiers come from them, Fulvius and the Essene voice their epitaphs for Spartacus and the vision of justice he had inherited: "He who receives the Word has a bad time of it. . . . He must carry it on and serve it in many ways, be they good or evil, until he may pass it on." The novel suggests that this race is unending, that it extends through history to include Koestler himself whose purpose is to bear witness to the necessity and the failure of revolutionary faith.

All of Koestler's novels are structured symmetrically, but nowhere is the technique more effectively used than in *The Gladiators*. Through the repetition of balanced sequences, the cycles of revolutionary experience develop a clear resonance within the structure itself. The entire action of the novel is framed by a Prologue and Epilogue, both focused on the meager day of Apronius, the Capuan clerk, which duplicate each other except for the varying of some details symbolic of the effect Spartacus has had on the Roman world. Each phase of the revolution is itself introduced by an "Interlude," again through the perspective of Apronius, or by a brief though highly evocative glimpse into the life of Hegio, an aristocratic citizen of Thurium.

In fact, both the arrival and departure of Spartacus are framed by the gracious, corrupt existence of this aesthete whose Greek ancestors built the city that is the foundation of the Sun State. By balancing Apronius and Hegio at opposite ends of the social spectrum, by implicitly comparing their political attitudes, their daily lives and fears, Koestler provides a specific and thoroughly recognizable focus for the revolution. Spartacus's just state is not simply an abstract conception born from parables and myth; it is a demand for concrete change rooted in a society whose only harmony is the decay of all its parts.

Apronius's reactions to Spartacus fluctuate as

dramatically as the price of corn. When his hopes for advancement are strong, he condemns the gladiator's threat to civilization. When, however, he becomes aware of his economic vulnerability, he envisions Spartacus as the scourge of Rome's corrupt leaders. Either reaction is characterized by his inability to move beyond himself, to perceive the world apart from his digestive problems. Indeed, he believes that "the majority of all rebellious discontent and revolutionary fanaticism are actually caused by an irregular digestion, or, to be more exact, by chronic constipation." Although he longs for a dictator who will care for "the little man," his spite and poverty of feeling actually perpetuate the debased status quo.

Hegio's perceptiveness and sophisticated humor make him far more agreeable as a character, yet in some basic respects he closely resembles Apronius. Hegio's sensitivity is languorous and detached, but concentrated on physical pleasures. He has great difficulty sustaining any perspective that is not dominated by his own ego. Through him Koestler draws one of the novel's most important contemporary associations. Hegio recognizes that corrupt and senseless as his society has become, "The forces of perseverance are tenacious." This tenacity—and one inevitably thinks of the hidden resilience of Western capitalism in the 1930s and 1940s—is created by the Italian population's "group-psychology," its inertia and deference to authority, and by the unchanging self-interest of individuals as divergent as Apronius, Hegio, and the various businessmen we encounter through them.

In the Epilogue, after Spartacus has been killed in battle, the novel returns to the squalid regularity of Apronius's day. Despite his culpability, we are compelled to sympathize with his loss of office and the breakdown of his skill as a scribe. But his aging, the simple encroachments of time on the pattern of his life, are set against the loss of what little freedom the slaves of Capua had before the Slave Revolt. In the Prologue Apronius was scornful of leaving the municipal slaves unchained. Now they are manacled again, their faces marked with hatred, and his response is unchecked fear. But a more subtle and benign change has occurred. Apronius sees in the midst of these slaves "the man in the fur-skin, with the sword in his hand." Spartacus's substantial, if barely willed accomplishment, is in the realm of the political imagination. He had already grown into legendary proportions; there are rumors that he did not really die, that he rose from the grave. He had become part of Apronius's nightmares and a figure in the mythological structure of revolution, a parable of the human need to believe in justice and equality.

When Koestler began to investigate the story of Spartacus, only its exotic and "romantic aspects" caught his interest. Soon, however, his concern "shifted from the picturesque facade to the historical and moral lessons of the first great proletarian revolution."[6] *The Gladiators*, the novels of Howard Fast, Evelyn Waugh's *Helena*, and William Golding's *The Spire*, while representing a wide range of literary merit, are all informed by the assumption that "the past will show the way mankind has gone and the direction in which it is moving."[7] The use of history as symbol, the impulse to draw parallels and to emphasize prefigurations—whether they are political, religious, or privately moral—differentiates these novels from the kind of historical fiction written by Robert Graves, the purpose of which is to re-create and illuminate on its own terms a certain period in the past.

Despite the increasing reputation of *The Gladiators* and the potential advantages of spatial and temporal distance for the expression of political ideas, Koestler said that he would never attempt another historical novel. The difficulty of projecting himself into the minds of representatives of an ancient civilization, what Peter Green has called the "empathic technique," was too onerous and ultimately restricting.[8] But it was a challenge to which Koestler responded with great literary intelligence. For example, he felt he had resolved the problem of portraying his inevitably alien characters by "modernizing" the members of Roman society and by delineating the gladiators themselves as "silhouettes in profile."[9] Although his purpose was to depict the dilemmas of revolutionary leadership, he was also committed to the aesthetics of the historical novel and the more general duty of the novelist to create genuine characters and events.

Analogies between the gladiators' uprising and the Russian Revolution abound in the novel, but his "contemporary bias" does not detract substantially from the sense of authenticity in Koestler's evocation of the period, which is in considerable measure established by the highly selective and intelligent use of detail or the suggestion of detail.[10] Koestler remarks that most of the information he accumulated about life at the time was not finally included in the novel, a welcome omission for readers who identify historical fiction with a flood of minutiae.[11] He seemed to grasp intuitively that the display of encyclopedic knowledge about an age reduces the credibility of the historical framework. The incessant intrusion of detail points to the author's self-consciousness rather than the period itself, and the reader's necessarily tenuous bond with a distant time is seriously disturbed.

But Koestler's maneuvering within the world of the Romans is performed with grace and precision. Although he does not directly describe Roman clothing, except as objects of Apronius's envy, the mention of the way he re-pleats his garment every night is an unobtrusively effective contribution to the historical reality. Similarly, the tenement in which he lives, the fire-escape he must climb daily, the cremation society he joins, his ritualistic bath, though noted only briefly, have behind them the weight of Koestler's knowledge of ordinary life during the period.

The political emphases of the novel also illustrate the principle that details are important as tools within the historical narrative and should have no exotically independent life of their own. The conservatism of Egnatus, the Senior Councillor of Nola, is conveyed largely in terms of an aging aristocrat's love for a precious vase. "He attempted to explain the difference between antique Etruscan or Cretan vases, and the modern mass-products from Samos and Arezzo." The vase, because it represents the traditional, aristocratic values of Rome, is the Councillor's ultimate argument against the more modern social theories expressed by his dinner guests. What Koestler discovered about these artifacts has no separate importance in the scene; the details are used not only to heighten the general sense of Roman life but also to provide a clear focus for the political debate among the enemies of the Slave revolt.

The difference in character between the Celts and the Thracians, the two major groups in the army, is handled in much the same way. Koestler does not merely inform us that the Celts are "moody, irascible creatures," whereas the Thracians are more united, mystical, and humane. These characteristics emerge throughout the narrative in the daily actions of each tribe. The conflict between Crixus and Spartacus— which ostensibly causes the revolution's failure and which is meant to be a clash of political types—is specifically related to national traits the credibility and vitality of which are established early in the novel, before the moral dilemmas are tightly patterned. The desire for freedom which, through the Essene, Spartacus builds into a city and system of laws, is firmly rooted in

the Thracians' memory of their existence in the mountains. Like the best political literature (Conrad's *Nos-
tromo*, Silone's *Fontamara*, Orwell's *Homage to Cata-
lonia*), *The Gladiators* moves to avoid an overemphasis
upon abstract ideology by underscoring the comprehensible details of common experience.

Whereas Koestler's penetration into facets of the
Roman world is both assured and compelling, his grasp
of the complexities of historical language is much less
certain. One of the major difficulties faced by historical
novelists is the choice of style or styles for the presenta-
tion of dialogue and descriptive narration. An unmodi-
fied modern diction tends to make the reader's ties with
his own time more immediate, which diminishes his
disinterested response to images of another, probably
quite different era. Indulgence in verbal antiques func-
tions in essentially the same manner. The studied un-
familiarity of language and syntax interposes the novelist's presence as maker between the reader and the
potential vitality and self-containment of the historical
period.[12]

*The Gladiators* displays a variety of styles and
approaches that are rarely harmonized. Koestler seems
to wander with vigorous unconcern from colloquial-
isms with a distinctly British-pub flavor to a ponder-
ously formalized diction complete with inversions, and
from the graves of the biblical prophets to a more
restrained, straightforward prose that implicitly and
effectively admits the modernity of the author. There is
no underlying rationale for this diversity, and the result
is often a fluctuation of styles within a single paragraph
or between consecutive sentences. Detailing the punishment of millwork, Koestler writes: "Gradually his
eyes grow sightless with all the dust and steam; and an
iron wheel is forged around his neck so that he cannot
put his hand to his mouth and taste of the flour. In this
manner Naso would soon have pegged out, although
not he but the steward was the real culprit."

But when the Essene is uttering his prophecies and parables, the novel's highly eccentric manner has a curious resonance. After Spartacus has received his visions of justice and righteousness, he says: "He who receives them will see evil days." The Essene replies: "Aye . . . he'll have a pretty rotten time." The implicit mockery in this change of language makes the encounter more human than mythical. The overblown, archaic expressions of prophecy are deflated, and Spartacus is temporarily reduced from a self-important apocalyptic figure to a revolutionary messenger, one among many in the historical pattern of revolt and failure.

The Essene tells a number of parables about God's spite and willfulness. Having bungled the creation of man and the animals, "to save His face He announced that it was His law which decreed that all living creatures should eat up each other. . . . Anyone, of course, can order things in such a way, there's nothing to it." What makes these parables so effective, perhaps the most effective ones in Koestler's fiction, is their integration with the novel as a whole and the ambiguity they represent in the Essene's attitudes. The jumps in style make us wonder whether he actually believes in such a God or even in the value of his own prophecies. Yet at the same time within his laconic, jagged remarks is a powerful current of anger, indignation, and sorrow at the condition of man on earth.

Koestler has stressed an essential advantage that the historical novel may have and which is denied to political novels dealing with events of the present. "If some critics have called it my best novel, it is perhaps because the passions and angers which contemporary events aroused in me were here projected on a screen remote in space and time, and purified from the topical dross which tends to clutter up my other books."[13] The distancing of perspective, the narrowing of emotion, results in certain kinds of reduction a reader would find antipathetic in an immediate, realistic narrative. Whereas unsophisticated, stark ideas about man and society would cheapen a novel about, for example, the Moscow purge trials or the holocaust, they are entirely compatible with the actions of gladiators and do not violate the reader's expectations.

Historical situations may also provide the political novelist with a unique latitude in terms of a character's intellectual and emotional resonance. A political novel about the present or the recent past must, to use Irving Howe's description, "contain the usual representation of human behavior and feeling; yet it must also absorb into its stream of movement the hard and perhaps insoluble pellets of modern ideology."[14] In *The Gladiators*, Koestler accepts this imperative, but largely restricts the complex interplay of "human behavior" and political idea to the representatives of the society against which Spartacus revolts. In this sense the Senators, military leaders, and businessmen of Capua and Rome are much like characters in a political narrative shaped by traditional realism. But the gladiators themselves have a simplicity of feeling and attitude, a limited consciousness of themselves, which is appropriate to a situation essentially unfamiliar to the reader. One invariably tries to share in the evocation of a distant, alien world and does not expect the same density of psychological nuance as in a novel by Dostoevsky or Conrad.

The distance that underlies *The Gladiators'* richness as history is best exhibited in the portrayal of Spartacus. Koestler's approach is marked by control, sensitivity, and a novelist's instinctive realization that a "world-historical individual," in George Lukács's phrase, should not be brought too close to the reader or allowed to remain in the foreground of the action.[15] He is a Thracian, but Koestler refrains from increasing our knowledge of his background. He possesses great influence not only over the physical environment of Italy but also over the imaginations of his followers and enemies alike. Yet, apart from the early moments of the revolt, he is seen very rarely and almost never in moments of solitary reflection, while his power is greatest during the creation of the Sun State when he virtually disappears from the direct action of the novel. By distancing him from the other characters and from the reader, Koestler sustains a personal mystery that is not only consistent with what we are unable to know about the past but which is also a measure of the dominance a political vision can exercise over the private self.

Even the record of his appearance adds to the sense of distance. Spartacus has a remarkable smile, but not until the final stages of his leadership are we informed that he is bearded. While providing a few physical characteristics—almost as if a full picture would make him too familiar, comprehensible—Koestler renders him in an unchanging pose, repeated throughout the novel: "He had a wide, good-natured face with many freckles all over it; his angular limbs, and the way he sat, ponderous elbows propped on his knees, made him look rather like a woodcutter of the mountains." When the burdens of his political decisions increase, he becomes more expressionless, but the pose remains fixed. The image suggests a statue, his permanence in the world, and at the same time his personal existence in the mountains from which his wrath and passion somehow grew.

But Spartacus did not suddenly and inexplicably accept an explosive commitment. Without explaining his motives in any detail, Koestler implies that Spartacus is thoroughly prepared for the Essene's cryptic prophecies of a secular Messiah.[16] Immediately after the escape from the circus, he shows a feeling of community, a sense of duty that is open to definition, and like the other Thracians, a profound instinct for freedom. "I have never been in Alexandria," he says before the encounter with the Essene. "It must be a very beautiful

place. Once I lay with a girl, and she sang. That is what
Alexandria must be like. Go on, Crixus, go and let your
phallus rove." The girl's soft song represents a personal
fulfillment denied to Crixus, and indeed most of Koestler's heroes. Because of this inner completion, the temptation to evade his publicness by escaping to Alexandria
has no great strength, and Spartacus is soon absorbing
all the legends of doomed revolt. He is already exhibit-
ing an energy that transcends the individual.

Had Koestler been able to sustain this exceptional
instinct for the demands of his subject, *The Gladiators*
might have had an almost incomparable power. But
Koestler's profound disaffection with the Party's morality could not, it seems, be fully satisfied by allegiance to
aesthetic principles and the nature of the narrative.
Because his anxiety about the present remained so
intense, despite the distant "mirror" that the historical
material provided, he had to be certain that all the
implications about revolutionary inspiration and corruption would be thoroughly understood. The consequence is that he temporarily confuses the reader's
perspective on Spartacus. Although we have come to
see him as a figure belonging to his time, many of his
later actions have distinctly Stalinist markings.

The debate that split the Soviet hierarchy in the
1930s was between those who insisted that the goal of a
Marxist revolution in Europe could not be compromised and those who argued for the primacy of a secure
base for the revolution in Russia. The culmination of the
debate was the German-Soviet Pact of 1939 that rup-
tured the already strained belief of countless fellow-
travelers and Party members throughout the world.
"Our allies will have nothing to fear from us," Fulvius
announces in the novel. The treaty with Thurium and
the negotiations for an alliance with the pirates are exact
echoes of Stalin's policies and the defeat of the "Trotsky-
ite" opposition.

Besides indulging in the symbols of an absolute ruler, Spartacus also displays the supreme trait of the dictator consumed by a messianic ideology—the assumption of historical infallibility: "He who guides the blind may not fear his own pride; he must make them suffer for their own good. For he alone can see while they are blind. There must be but *one* will, the will of the knowing." While the Sun State is in existence, the reader's process of association remains disjointed since Koestler emphasizes both the specific, contemporary meaning of an act or attitude and the historical reality of his characters' world. Crixus is consistent with his age even more solidly than Spartacus; he is a melancholy, brutal hedonist to whom the idea of a just commonwealth is incomprehensible. Yet Koestler's insistence on his Russian "silhouettes" demands that we consider the identification of Crixus and Trotsky, if only to reject it. The "dissident" Celts do not present an ideological alternative to Spartacus, only a baser style of life.

There are, however, instances in the novel when Koestler's preoccupation with modern meanings is dynamically balanced with the historical perspective. During the siege of Capua by the gladiators' army, Fulvius witnesses in the patriotic fervor of the poor a frightening susceptibility to propaganda and group impulse. Gradually, the description of the Capuan masses becomes less timebound and begins to suggest other images—of an impoverished German public's response to clarions of heredity, to new symbols and a shrill voice proclaiming a revitalized destiny. "The last one to try saving this putrid order had been Sulla. . . . Only those who could prove that the blood in their veins was that of the superior She-Wolf-Race were to be the Lords and Masters in this state; every one else was as nothing before him." Recorded by a character who is as yet detached from the political action, this reflection of prewar Germany arises from the movement of the novel itself, whereas the analogies with Soviet communism seem to be imprints of the author's sense of personal urgency.

In his memoirs, essays, and conversation, Koestler reiterated that after his months awaiting execution in Spain, questions of political morality became the "central concern" of his writing. *The Gladiators* and *Darkness at Noon* were designed as "variations on the same theme: the problem of Ends and Means, the conflict between transcendental morality and social expediency."[17] The "variations" are in the nature of the plot and the protagonist. The conflict itself remains fixed, apparently closed to redefinition by the ambiguities of choice or consciousness. In the first novels one is either brutal and politically effective or, by being possessed of human feeling, responsible for the failure of the revolution. Stark as Koestler intends to make the dilemma in *The Gladiators*, it is not obvious that Spartacus is caught between the extremes of violence and inaction, that his revolution depends upon an awesome act of cruelty.

Moreover, Koestler's success in making the Celts historically credible again proves problematic for the novel's moral scheme. Spartacus's decision to force a split in the Slave Army may be seen as a violent "detour," an exercise in political expediency, since he knows that the smaller group under Crixus will likely be slaughtered by a Roman legion. But as an example of absolute moral choice, as a decision central to the novel's conception of revolutionary authority, the issue is muted by the way the reader has perceived the Celts throughout. They are a destructive force devoid of social understanding and human compassion. As Orwell recognized, their violence, which prompts Spartacus's strategy, cannot be regarded as revolutionary or counterrevolutionary; at best it is vengeance against their

former overlords, at worst an irrepressible form of barbaric fun.[18] The Celts belong entirely and authentically
to a world of instinct and unconsidered power. Within
the narrative—as distinct from the purpose Koestler
wants to give the narrative—Spartacus is virtually a
humanitarian in not wishing to inflict Crixus on mankind. Furthermore, most of the "offenders" welcome
the separation, despite their physical danger.

One's sense of Koestler's rigidity of conception is
confirmed by the sequence of events that leads to this
first detour. In his mind Spartacus "had walked the
straight road" from the moment he inspired the slaves
with the vision of justice and equality. But there is no
description of this phase of his leadership at all; the
raping and ravaging seem to have started the instant
Spartacus stopped speaking to his followers in the
crater of Mount Vesuvius. The moral geography of
straight and twisted roads that begins to haunt him here
is not only dubious but also hurriedly imposed. The
detours later become an abyss. Crixus drunkenly wonders whether he should inspect the sentries: "One
should curse their vices—one's own; should condemn
their greed—one's own; deny their drunkenness—one's
own drunkenness. One should obey the law of detours."
A weighty question of social ethics has come to be
almost meaningless. Deviousness is equated with the
simplest kind of order, whereas directness, the "straight
road," apparently signifies the unexamined exercise of
whim.

The other major examples of the conflict between
ends and means are not as prone to the corruption of
terms. When Spartacus invites the treaty with Thurium
and renounces the claim of brotherhood on its slaves, he
is making an unmistakable detour from the direct pursuit of revolution. The decision to purify the Sun State
of its Celtic "infection" is an equally clear acceptance of
revolutionary violence. There is no alternative at this

point but to resort to the terror that is the underside of absolute power. But one encounters an even more fundamental problem here than Koestler's impatience or carelessness with language.

Koestler ascribes the entire failure of the revolution to Spartacus's retreat from the necessary bloodletting. But no revolution perishes as a consequence of a single act or nonact. From what we have seen of Spartacus's leadership, his refusal to order the massacre is only the final detail in an already impossible adventure. The collapse of the Sun State is also the result of his aloofness from the common people, his inability to erode the conventional equation between freedom and total leisure, and, most important, his inability to provide the essential dynamic of revolution—a comprehensive and resilient faith. Crassus's analysis is basically accurate: "If your intentions were serious, you should have invented a new religion which . . . raised labour to the station of a creed and cult, and declared sweat to be ambrosia." But Spartacus insists that priests and a new religion were not necessary, that all his followers required was land.

His naiveté extends to his dealings with the leaders of Thurium. Spartacus holds to the letter of the treaty while the narrator is at pains to emphasize the cunning and dishonesty of the town's ruling group in deliberately instigating the food shortage and planting the idea that neighboring Metapontum is rich and open to attack. Spartacus does not feel that the revolution is sufficiently threatened to pressure Thurium, to wield simply the threat of violence. For the sake of his moral design, Koestler has not permitted Spartacus to understand that the "law of detours" applies to various levels of political behavior, that it is not limited to the use of absolute terror.

Koestler is intent upon proving, as Jenni Calder notes, that because of the tension between humanity and an authority confirmed by violence, "the revolutionary leader is an impossibility."[19] Yet in thinking about his people, Spartacus acknowledges the potential existence of different revolutionary leaderships:

> No, one could neither guide it from outside nor from above, not with the pride of the lonely seer, nor with the cunning of detours, nor with the cruel kindness of the prophet. The century of abortive revolutions had been completed; others will come, receive the word and pass it on in a great wrathful relay-race through the ages; and from the bloody birth-pangs of revolution again and again a new tyrant will be born—until at last the groaning human clod would itself begin to think with its thousand heads; until knowledge was no longer foisted on it from outside, but was born in laboured torment out of its own body, thus gaining from within power over the happening.

The experience of Spartacus is therefore authoritarian and proves only that external control and legislation cannot guarantee the permanence of a vision of justice. Whether or not a proletariat giving birth to its own consciousness can be more fruitful is another question entirely. All one can conclude is that, despite the universality of his original impulse and the continuity of the quest for justice, Spartacus's leadership is limited to its historical context and defined by its social assumptions. The energy of the Sun City is dissipated through inadequate awareness, not through moral absoluteness.

The usual criticism of Koestler as a novelist is that he subordinates the art of fiction to the urgency of his political ideas. In fact, the falterings of *The Gladiators* and *Darkness at Noon* are intellectual, and their power is chiefly aesthetic. The narrative shape, the preparation of the hero for ideological surgery, is masterful, but tremendous strains on the texture of each novel are created by Koestler's moral intransigence, by the dominance that a single attitude can have over his understanding of political experience and the literary demands of the subject. His ideas remained immutable principles, and he remained a writer at odds with himself.

# 3

## The Mind on Trial:
*Darkness at Noon*

Completing *The Gladiators* had helped Koestler bear the sense of "outer loneliness and inner emptiness" he experienced in finally choosing to dislocate his personal history from that of the Communist Revolution.[1] But as a novelist, a reporter, and an individual whose very pulse seemed to be political, Koestler's instinct was to stay closer to the ideological convulsions of his own time, among the legacies of a bankrupt rationalism he saw embodied in Marxism. With his second novel Koestler turned from the relative comfort of historical emblems to the painful and immediate moral pressure exerted on the European Left by the Moscow Trials, Stalin's systematic and precisely orchestrated burial of the Bolshevik "old guard."

The novel was originally called *The Vicious Circle* and was to center on a group of characters imprisoned in a totalitarian state. The real guilt they share, Koestler says in the autobiography, is "having placed the interests of mankind above the interests of man, having sacrificed morality to expediency. . . . Now they must die, because their death is expedient to the Cause, by the hands of men who subscribe to the same principles."[2] In the actual writing of the novel, Koestler held to this conflict between means and ends, but of the figures he planned to include, only one grew in his imagination—Nikolai Salmanovich Rubashov—whose "manner of thinking" was modeled on that of Nikolai Bukharin, the most notable defendant in the Great Trial of 1938. Intellectually the most fascinating of the Bolshevik leaders, Bukharin had been "a ranking member of Lenin's original revolutionary leadership," the editor of *Pravda*, "and co-leader with Stalin of the Party between 1925 and 1928."[3]

Although during his own trial Rubashov echoes some of Bukharin's most eloquent words, his ancestry is also more general. In an important sense Rubashov represents an entire generation of "militant philosophers" who by the early 1930s had few resources left to withstand Stalin and Stalinism. What Koestler remembered most about the various members of the Soviet hierarchy he met in 1933, including Bukharin, was their fatigue:

> It was not only the effect of overwork, nervous strain and apprehension. It was the past that was telling on them, the years of conspiracy, prison and exile; the years of the famine and the Civil War; and sticking to the rules of a game that demanded that at every moment a man's whole life should be at stake. They were indeed "dead men on furlough," as Lenin had called them. Nothing could frighten them any more, nothing surprise them. They had given all they had. History had squeezed them out to the last drop, had burnt them out to the last spiritual calorie; yet they were still glowing in cold devotion, like phosphorescent corpses.[4]

They had not yet given everything; there was still to be a claim on their "cold devotion." Between 1935 and 1938 they and the rest of the revolutionary elite, the creators of the 1917 Revolution, confessed in open court to being saboteurs, assassins, thieves, and agents of foreign powers. The trials bewildered and frightened observers, those on the independent Left, fellow travelers, and Communist Party members throughout the world. If the accused were guilty, a generation of Bolshevik politicians and whole sections of Russian revolutionary history were tainted. If they were innocent, the current Soviet leadership was dedicated to a program of baroque vengeance and self-interest wholly incompatible with anything but the most dogmatic, inhumane revolutionary principles. After Koestler's death, the philosopher Sidney Hook remarked that only "*Darkness at Noon* was able to convey the sickening truth, overcoming by its psychological plausibility the initial doubts and resistance of Communist sympathisers."[5]

In his essay on Koestler, Orwell argued that "the common-sense explanation" for the confessions was that the accused "were tortured, and perhaps blackmailed by threats to relatives and friends."[6] Koestler did not discount this sort of pressure. In the novel itself and in numerous debates about Rubashov, Koestler agreed that some confessed in the hope of saving their families or their own lives. But in Rubashov Koestler dramatized a more complex motive which for years after the publication of the book proved to be highly controversial. "The best of them, the hard-core Bolshevik intellectuals" behind the creation of Rubashov "were great men, and it would be the final injustice to misinterpret the motives for which they died." They confessed and died "to do the Party a last service."[7]

With the exception of a few scenes, *Darkness at Noon* is concentrated in the mind of ex-Commissar of the People Rubashov: his meditations on political ethics, his memories, his debates with the interrogators, and ultimately his decision to acquiesce in the Party's demand on him. In the opening section, "The First Hearing," Rubashov is arrested by his own countrymen. With a detachment that comes from years of self-abnegation and ideological commitment, he surveys his body, contemplates the possibility of his execution, and assesses the power of No. 1 (Stalin is never named in the book). Rubashov wonders whether "that

mocking oracle they called History" might prove that
No. 1 was correct in his decimation of the "old guard."

But the workings of his own history refuse to
remain so opaque. In the solitariness of prison Rubashov's memories become living presences. "The im-
ploring gesture of the meagre, stretched-out hands"
from a neighboring cell reminds him of a *Pietà* that
hung in a German gallery. As head of an Intelligence
unit, Rubashov had been sent to deal with "Richard," a
German Party worker who had been distributing
"defeatist" pamphlets. After explaining the need for
unwavering faith and obedience, Rubashov expelled
Richard from the Party and betrayed him to Hitler's
police. When he left the gallery, Rubashov was aware
not of guilt, but of a tormenting toothache.

This physical response, prompted by his rudimen-
tary conscience, becomes even more acute while Rubashov paces in his cell and begins to voice doubts about
the Party's infallibility: "We brought you truth and in
our mouth it sounded a lie. We brought you freedom,
and it looks in our hands like a whip." This meditation
extracts another painful recollection: his explantion to a
group of Belgian dockworkers that they should not
prevent the shipment of goods to a Fascist state, since
"the Country of the Revolution" had to increase its
industrial capacity, not encourage "romantic gestures."
The embargo was lifted, and after being "denounced in
the official Party organ as an *agent provocateur*," the
union leader, Little Loewy, hanged himself. Without
belief in the Revolution and its heroes, he could not
continue to live.

Between these memories Rubashov has conversations in code with his monarchist neighbor, No. 402,
from whom he receives unexpected tobacco and emotional generosity. But there remains more common
ground with his first official interrogator, Ivanov, an
old comrade Rubashov had once persuaded on ideolog-

ical grounds not to commit suicide. Ivanov points out that despite some reluctance, Rubashov has made various "declarations of loyalty" over the years in order to avoid expulsion from the Party. He argues that Rubashov's past and his need to remain within the Party logically dictate that he make a partial confession now. "The methods follow by logical deduction . . . and in five years you will be back in the ring again." Although Rubashov says that he has had "enough of this kind of logic," Ivanov "had hit a tuning fork, to which his mind responded of its own accord. All he had believed in, fought for and preached during the last forty years swept over his mind in an irresistible wave."

In "The Second Hearing" Rubashov begins to make the acquaintance of the "grammatical fiction," the illogical realm of selfhood and personal conscience that had been stifled by his habitual submission to political expediency. The "silent partner," as he also calls his inner voice, has already drawn him to certain images: to the *Pietà* that had been partly hidden from his view as he excommunicated Richard and to the cats Little Loewy was forced to skin in order to survive for the sake of the Party. Now, through the memory of his lover's bent neck, it draws Rubashov to his most complete betrayal. While working at a trade delegation in a European country, Rubashov lived for weeks "in the atmosphere of [Arlova's] large, lazy body." During the day and at night he found her sisterly, sensual warmth more human than anything he had encountered before in his life. But when Arlova was "recalled" and accused of treason, he neither came to her public defense nor did he attempt to comfort her in private. Rubashov's simple calculation was that his own existence was more valuable to the Party.

Joining these images within Rubashov's "first person singular" is the sound of Bogrov—"Former Sailor on the Battleship Potemkin, Commander of the Eastern

Fleet"—whimpering, crying for his old friend, as he is
led past Rubashov's cell. Even after this horrifying
example of No. 1's "objective" morality, Ivanov continues to argue that "sympathy, conscience, disgust,
despair, repentance, and atonement are for us repellent
debauchery." But Rubashov cannot throw him out,
cannot reject his entire past which is carried in this echo
of his own words and attitudes.

In "The Third Hearing" Rubashov proudly informs
Ivanov and No. 402 that he is capitulating. A general
recantation will, he has decided, allow him some
"breathing-space" as well as time to formulate new
theories of social utility and revolutionary ethics. But
Ivanov has himself been arrested and another interrogator installed. Representing a new, "Neanderthal"
generation, and sharing neither memories nor style with
the old intelligentsia, Gletkin demands from Rubashov
a complete public confession to crimes of treason and
espionage. "You admit your 'oppositional attitude,'" he
says to Rubashov, "but deny the acts which are the
logical consequence of it." Rubashov has insisted that
he cannot confess to crimes he has not committed. But
gradually he submits to what Koestler's friend Raymond Aron calls "the perverse logic of those chain
identifications . . . that are the essence, the diabolical
and fascinating essence of an absolute historical faith."[8]

Confronted with "Hare-lip," in whose presence
years earlier he had mocked and condemned the Soviet
leadership, Rubashov concludes that it is irrelevant
whether the young man actually tried to assassinate No.
1: "The essential point was that this figure of misery
represented the consequence of his logic made flesh."
When Rubashov acknowledges to Gletkin that Hare-
lip's confession "accords with the facts in the *essential*
points," he "seals" his own confession. Although he
could simplify the interrogation by admitting the entire
indictment all at once, Rubashov contests every point;

he must see the macabre dance of casuistical intellect
through to the very end. He has tacitly agreed that if
Gletkin could prove the accuracy of the "root" of a
charge—"even when this root was only of a logical,
abstract nature—he had a free hand to insert the missing
details. . . . Neither of them distinguished any longer
between actions which Rubashov had committed in
fact and those which he merely should have committed
as a consequence of his opinions." To complete the
logic of the interrogation and at the same time to secure
his bond with the past, Rubashov agrees to a ritualistic
trial as his "last service" to the Revolution.

"The Grammatical Fiction" begins with an account
of the public confession. Virtually every perception
and thought in the novel has been Rubashov's, yet the
trial, toward which he has inexorably argued himself
and the elite of the "old guard," is conveyed through a
newspaper description read to the porter, Vassilij.
Denying Rubashov the direct narration of the event is
remarkably effective. He has, in essence, relinquished
both the ethical and aesthetic right to speak for himself.
His perverse rationalism has temporarily canceled what
individuality he possessed, and for the duration of the
trial he is nothing more or less than a public creation of
the Party. As a result, his direct reactions to the charges
of the prosecution and the jeers of the audience are
sadly irrelevant.

Having made his peace with history, Rubashov is
free to contemplate the "grammatical fiction" and the
questions it evokes about human suffering. He goes to
his death unsure that there is any difference between
No. 1 and the German messiah, but in the hope that
perhaps a "new movement" will arise, driven by
knowledge of both "economic fatality" and the "oceanic feeling" (the sense of infinity Koestler himself glimpsed
while under sentence of death in Spain and which he
called on again in his suicide note). "Perhaps," Ruba-

shov thinks, "the members of the new party will wear monks' cowls, and preach that only purity of means can justify the ends."

But it was as a weapon, not as an expression of hope, that the book had such an extraordinary influence when the translation, *Le Zéro et l'Infini* appeared in France. Koestler maintains that the reason the book "broke all prewar records in French publishing history was not literary but political."[9] In 1946 the French Communist Party was extremely powerful, well-organized, and likely to increase its governmental control through a constitutional referendum. "In this oppressive atmosphere, a novel on the Russian Purges, though dealing with events that lay ten years back, assumed a symbolic actuality, an allusive relevance which had a deeper psychological impact than a topical book could have achieved. It happened to be the first moral indictment of Stalinism published in post-war France."[10]

Judging from the shrill attacks on Koestler's manhood and drinking habits as well as his "graveyard" politics, the novel produced considerable distress among the Party orthodox.[11] At the same time, it confirmed others in their anticommunism and swayed the uncommitted *either* toward or away from the Party. This paradoxical effect, which Koestler was very much aware of, but did not emphasize publicly, in his essays or autobiography, is rather startling evidence of his persuasive detailing of Bolshevik rationalism and argumentation. The novel also prompted in the eminent philosopher Maurice Merleau-Ponty an immediate and lengthy response to the concepts implicit in the portrayal of Rubashov. As a Marxist with little sympathy for Stalin's version of revolutionary terror, Merleau-Ponty believed that Koestler had at least approached the essential terms of contemporary political ethics: "Even if it does not pose the question properly, the book raises the problem of our times"—how to balance the human demands of social change with the inhuman temper of violence.[12]

Koestler cites the assertion in a Paris editorial that "the most important single factor which led to the defeat of the Communists in the referendum on the Constitution, was a novel, *Le Zéro et l'Infini.*"[13] Even if only partly accurate, this statement gives Koestler's novel a place in an uncrowded area of literary history, among works that have had a direct and verifiable effect on a society's approach to its structures and principles. *Darkness at Noon*, like *Nineteen Eighty-Four* and *Uncle Tom's Cabin*, became a catalyst of public opinion by accident. Passions about slavery and Soviet communism absorbed these novels in a particular way at the right, the necessary, historical moment. But Koestler could not plan this necessity or foresee the postwar compulsions of France. Although he *hoped* to affect his readers' understanding of Stalinism, he wrote *Darkness at Noon* as though he had to be content with the traditional significance of imaginative forms—the slow and subtle alteration of a culture's mode of perception.

Koestler's intention to mold the subject of Rubashov's confession into a fully integrated and permanent artistic entity is evident from the first pages of the novel. After Rubashov has examined his cell and fallen asleep, we are taken back to his arrest at home an hour earlier. He is straining to wake himself from the recurrent nightmare of his initial arrest by the Gestapo. "He dreamed, as always, that there was a hammering on his door, and that three men stood outside, waiting to arrest him." Then Koestler explicitly binds the dream to the present reality:

> The hammering on Rubashov's door became louder; the two men outside, who had come to arrest him, hammered alternatively and blew on their frozen hands. But Rubashov could not wake up, although he

knew that now would follow a particularly painful
scene: the three still stand by his bed and he tries to put
on his dressing-gown.

Vassilij, the old porter and Rubashov's follower, takes
part in the translation of the nightmare; he is the third
person standing by Rubashov's bed as he awakes.
Koestler's literary self-consciousness is clearly exhibited
here. Yet the deliberateness does not diminish the
exceptional intensity in the identification of Rubashov's
past and present.

Patterns of repetition and contrast are pursued
throughout the novel. For instance, Rubashov becomes
obsessed with the memory of a photograph of delegates to the First Party Congress. These men, among
whom he sat, "looked like the meeting of a provincial
town Council," yet "dreamed of power with the object
of abolishing power; of ruling over the people to wean
them from the habit of being ruled." Although the picture was once displayed prominently throughout the
country, in embassies as well as in prisons, now there
are only light patches on the walls. It epitomizes the
past that No. 1 has repudiated, but which Rubashov
cannot erase.

Rubashov reveres and is himself worshipped. To
Vassilij the official portrait of Rubashov as a commander in the Civil War is a sacred possession, but it too
must now be taken down and will survive only in the
memories of the old. When Rubashov is arrested, his
eyes have "the expression which Vassilij and the elder
official knew from old photographs and colour-prints."
Even the prison warder is reminded of "the colour-
prints of Rubashov in uniform, which in the old days
one used to see everywhere." Koestler's purpose is
again accomplished with considerable neatness and
precision. These memories interact with Rubashov's
own recollection of the Congress portrait to form an

extensive metaphoric structure that confirms his aliena-
tion from the present regime and course of the revolution.

But the bond between Rubashov and an ostensibly
more humane generation is not without qualification.
The Rubashov Vassilij worships is "the little bearded
Partisan commander who had known such beautiful
oaths that even the Holy Madonna of Kasan must have
smiled at them." The language of this Rubashov was
spontaneous and full of human feeling, but has been
abandoned for the grotesque and deadening rhetoric of
Party dialectics. After the Civil War, Vassilij found
Rubashov's formal Congress speeches nearly incomprehensible. Rubashov accuses the Party of forfeiting
its understanding of the masses, "the great silent x of
history," but because Vassilij, who represents this
abstract factor in the flesh, never impinges on Rubashov's consciousness, it is clear that the responsibility
belongs as much to Rubashov as to No. 1. Never does
Rubashov conceive of his past the way Vassilij
remembers it. The Party Congress and its vast design
plague him, not the long-dead vitality of his own
leadership.

Koestler's method of balancing characters in terms
of similarities and differences is also apparent in Rubashov's relationship with his interrogator, Gletkin.
Initially, despite the old Bolshevik's aversion to the
barbarism of the new generation, he tries to persuade
himself that the Gletkins must be accepted because
they have right on their side and represent a necessary
modification in the Party. When, during the investigation, Rubashov comes to reaffirm the supremacy of
reason and logical consequence, his attitude toward the
new breed alters. Gletkin is no longer an aberrant
necessity, but actually the creation of the old guard:
"Massive and expressionless, he sat there, the brutal
embodiment of the State which owned its very exist-

ence to the Rubashovs and Ivanovs. Flesh of their flesh, grown independent and become insensible." Koestler also links Gletkin with Vassilij: both of them, the narrative emphasizes, received scars in the Civil War. The inevitable implication is that even Vassilij's loyalty enabled the Bolsheviks to develop and fulfill their dictum, that the end, when political, justifies the means.

Koestler's highly self-conscious and compelling artistry is evident not only in his alignment of characters but also in the overall structure of the novel. The beginning of the novel introduces patterns, like the photographs and the equation of religious and ideological faith, which are sustained throughout, and at the end the prominent threads are tied together, the final symmetry formed. Awaiting his execution, Rubashov expresses his sense of defeat in biblical terms. Moses at least saw "the land of promise," whereas "he, Nicolai Salmanowitch Rubashov, had not been taken to the top of the mountain; and wherever his eye looked, he saw nothing but desert and the darkness of night." He imagines his own executioner exactly as he did Bogrov's: a dentist who conceals his tools in his sleeve. We are meant to recall that when Rubashov went to Germany to excommunicate Richard, he was disguised as a salesman of dental instuments and that every guilty association in his mind has been accompanied by a toothache.

The memory of his arrest in Gemany returns and with it the metaphorical identification of the Nazi and Soviet dictatorships. For the last time Rubashov smells fresh leather, a smell associated with the Gestapo agents, with the first chairman of the Communist International, and with Gletkin—a fraternity that for Koestler encompasses the horrors of European totalitarianism. Rubashov thinks he is back in his room and wonders "whose colour-print portrait was hanging over his bed and looking at him? Was it No. 1 or was it the other—he with the ironic smile or he with the glassy gaze?" In his autobiography Koestler says that the portraits of Stalin and Hitler appear at the beginning and end of the novel.[14] Curiously, the picture of Hitler is in fact described only once, in the instant before Rubashov's execution. One can only conclude that the symmetry of *Darkness at Noon* was intended to be even more complete.

But most readers have been less interested in the novel's narrative intricacies than in the validity of its psychological and historical interpretations. The Soviet dissident writer Alexander Solzhenitsyn has praised the novel as a "talented inquiry," which, more than any other document, has helped to clarify the "riddle" of the trials. He explains that Bukharin, the chief model for Rubashov, confessed out of total devotion to and need for the Party. "Bukharin (like all the rest of them) did not have his own *individual point of view*.[15] Yet in his political biography of Bukharin, Stephen Cohen argues that it was not a barren marriage with the soul of the Party that prompted his confession, but the hope of keeping his family alive. Cohen insists, moreover, that during the trial Bukharin managed to defend "Bolshevism's historical legacy."[16]

Literary critics, particularly those with a fundamental belief in the value of political literature, have also found Koestler's psychology "untrue to our sense of human behavior, even the behavior of Bolshevik politicians."[17] Indeed, it is true, as Irving Howe points out, that Koestler omits the "whole middle ground of Rubashov's experience, the gradual destruction of his will and integrity as he takes step after step toward acquiescing to the regime he knows to be vile."[18] This omission eventually calls into question Koestler's sense of history. But the process of the confession itself is not detached and "superimposed." Rubashov's unyielding belief in reason emerges in all his actions, and by the

time of the last interrogations, we come to expect
nothing from him but the most rigid, self-justifying
logicality.

Before raising the issue of the confession, Koestler
very skillfully depicts Rubashov's temperament in a
variety of its manifestations. Rather than eliciting shock
or fear, the arrest and imprisonment trigger Rubashov's
habitual reliance upon his powers of logical analysis. He
meets every detail of the situation with self-congratulatory expertise. When we first see him, he is
inspecting his cell and making a mental inventory. He
assesses the resonance of the walls and pipes: "So far
everything was in order."

But Koestler weaves ironies into his responses,
even during these early stages of isolation. Rubashov
has correctly deduced that it is improbable "one had to
get up here before seven in winter." Soon he hears
marching in the corridors and expects the various sorts
of torture to begin. Yet his anxiety is suddenly deflated
by the appearance of "two orderlies dragging a tub of
tea." Similarly, having fallen asleep in apparent control
of himself and what is being done to him, Rubashov
cannot will the movements of his hand. The real control
is held by the guards who watch him twitch in his sleep.
The arrival of the tea and the spasms of his hand are
brief but powerful notations of the frailty at the heart of
Rubashov's rational belief in himself.

There is no room in his makeup for unmitigated
fear or prolonged surprise. The first scream of the tortured was usually terrible, he reminds himself, but then
"one got used to it and after a time one could even draw
conclusions on the method of torture from the tone and
rhythm of the screams." Whereas this assessment is an
evocative balance of human self-protectiveness and an
almost inhuman reliance on reason and empirical data,
his code-contacts with No. 402 demonstrate the self-
deception, the absurd *hubris*, in his readiness to draw an
idea out to its logical conclusion.

When No. 402 refuses his request for tobacco, Rubashov retreats into a precise, visual judgment of the monarchist prisoner: "He saw the young officer with the small moustache, the monocle stuck in, staring with a stupid grin at the wall which separated them." Comforted by this image, he deduces that between "you and us there is no common currency and no common language." But his proud logic crumbles because No. 402 suddenly decides to send some tobacco and because we realize that Rubashov had constructed his picture of an archetypal class enemy through a faulty process of logical inference. The monocle and moustache were hypothetical details that instantly became fixed in Rubashov's mind, made absolute by his syllogistic obsessions.

The pathos of his devout rationalism is also apparent in Rubashov's reactions to Arlova and Gletkin. After she is dismissed from her post, she desperately wants Rubashov to say or do something to affirm their bond; all he can sense is some urgency, but nothing of what it means. As a result, it is a relatively uncomplex decision for him to choose his own political survival over her life. But Rubashov has as much difficulty sustaining hate as love. His revulsion from Gletkin vanishes as soon as he lapses into the eminently rational habit of placing himself in his opponent's position. This tendency, which both annoys Rubashov and yet is the source of an eccentric pride, is highly selective. He can project himself into another's mind only if its perceptions are similar to his own. Because of their commitment to logical expediency, Gletkin and Ivanov, to some extent even No. 1, are open to his sensibility whereas the more emotional Arlova, Richard, and Little Loewy are essentially alien creatures to him.

Because Rubashov is an incomplete human being, even his discovery of guilt and selfhood is appallingly frail. The "closed system mentality" is so deeply rooted in him that his questioning and ultimately his renunciation of reason are either kept on the level of fragmentary memories or made abstract by being expressed in the language of reason. Jenni Calder remarks: "Even his doubts are sifted, categorised, channelled, by the habit of logical thought."[19] No genuine difference develops between Rubashov's articulation of his groping toward individuality, the claims of personal self, and the opposite side of the dilemma, the argument that feelings, privacy, and conscience are irrelevant to the inexorable sweep of the revolution. The rigid predictability of Rubashov's intellect erodes any hope we have for a fundamental change in his character.

The irony and sadness of his perceptions are most intense when he begins to reflect upon "the grammatical fiction," the realm of subjective reality. Forty years of political devotion and human denial have eliminated the use of "I" from his vocabulary. As a result, he is "shy" in the presence of his hidden self, ashamed to confront it directly: hence, the peculiar terminology. Initially Rubashov searches for the meaning of "the silent partner" with the impersonal curiosity that an unexpected problem in logistics or the appearance of something unusual under the microscope might arouse:

> He found out that those processes wrongly known as "monologues" are really dialogues of a special kind; dialogues in which one partner remains silent while the other, against all grammatical rules, addresses him as "I" instead of "you", in order to creep into his confidence and to fathom his intentions; but the silent partner just remains silent, shuns observation and even refuses to be localized in time and space.

There is an excitement and appropriateness in Rubashov's clinical appraisal of this novel sense of irrationality. The reader is bound to hope that the molecular vision will grow and reshape itself into an all-encompassing meditation. But Rubashov ultimately responds to the promptings of the inner voice with an unconscious process of classification. Because he is reluctant to defile the personal self by open contact with the facts of revolutionary violence and paradoxically because at the same time they threaten the validity of his past, Rubashov transfers his guilt-ridden memories to a sealed psychological vault where they remain until his transaction with the Party is complete.

The inevitability of Rubashov's confession is concentrated in the novel's most powerful episode, the scenes surrounding Bogrov's execution. One evening Rubashov senses "something unusual in the air" and is told that executions of his "sort" are imminent. With each detail passed from cell to cell, the intensity and Rubashov's awareness of his senses become unbearably acute. He wants the name of the victim and is finally told, "BOGROV. OPPOSITIONAL. PASS IT ON." We are not given Rubashov's reactions directly. To his neighbor he taps out his friend's full name, his distinction in the Revolution, and his fate. As Bogrov is carried before the cells, the prisoners' drumming grows to hypnotic force, and for an instant Rubashov ceases to be chained by his rigid intellectual patterns. He becomes, like the others, a primitive being pounding on the bars to reclaim part of himself lost to the shadows of political clarity.

But the essential horror is less in the image of Bogrov than in Rubashov's readiness to stop hearing the sound of his friend's broken voice. Barely minutes after the prisoners' tribal farewell, Rubashov again begins to argue with Ivanov: "He felt dully that the conversation had taken a turn which he should not have allowed . . . he had not thrown out Ivanov. That alone, it seemed to him, was a betrayal of Bogrov—and of Arlova; and of Richard and Little Loewy." Even this perception cannot withstand the power Ivanov wields. Using many of Rubashov's own phrases, his appeal to Rubashov's past and his habitual logicality is bound to be effective because it evokes what is most deeply rooted in him. And Rubashov is not prepared to face the chaos and historical degradation that keeping silent would entail.

After the trial Rubashov turns again to the "silent partner" and frees it from its chaste isolation. Yet he still approaches it with the eye of an ideologue and welcomes it in the language that had voiced his "treason." "Obviously, only such suffering made sense, as was inevitable; that is, as was rooted in biological fatality." He has a vague glimpse of the eternal, but this too is cast in the abstract. Even his hope for the emergence of a "new movement" is expressed in predominantly mathematical terms; perhaps its members "will introduce a new kind of arithmetic based on multiplication." Rubashov's worthiest, most humane ideas are absorbed, pathetically altered, by a process of thought associated with cruelty.

The essential problem with *Darkness at Noon* is not aesthetic. The preparation for the confession is handled with great narrative skill. In his responses to prison and the past, Rubashov is one of the finest creations in modern political literature. But he is not a complete character. Out of a peculiar intellectual rigidity of his own, Koestler dooms Rubashov to an absolute dichotomy between historical belief and personal conscience.[20] He is not allowed to strive for their integration and reach a dead end. He is made to assume their eternal distinctness. There is no "middle ground of his experience," no change detailed within the narrative from Vassilij's Partisan commander to the betrayer of Richard and Arlova, because it seems that for Koestler purpose is instantly corrupted by method. What shapes the novel is not a conception of historical process, but an extraordinary ethical fatalism.

During the initial interrogation conducted by Ivanov, Rubashov says that his disillusionment with the course of the Revolution developed in "the last few

years," at the time, that is, when he was driving dissident Party members to suicide or execution. But in the
scene with Richard he is not shown to be conscious of
any doubts about the Party's forging of historical
change. Since the image of the *Pietà* and the paintings
of human sensuality he sees in the gallery do not directly
affect Rubashov's thinking, we must assume that he still
believes the arguments he presents to his ideological
victim with all the passion of the zealot.

The portrayal of his Belgian mission is similar. Listening to a dockworker who, like Richard, has arrived
at the painful realization that "the Party is becoming
more and more fossilized," Rubashov thinks: "I could
tell you more about it." It would be understandable if
he were merely unwilling to take the strike leader into
his confidence. But Rubashov cannot sustain a *private*
awareness of his uncertainties: "he was again fully convinced of the necessity and utility of his mission and
could not understand why, in the noisy pub the night
before, he had had that feeling of uneasiness." And
again Rubashov completes his task with no further hesi-
tation or reluctance.

The problem with these episodes is that Rubashov
is not allowed to act in the interests of the Party and out
of his years of commitment to the Revolution while also
being aware of fundamental doubts about the validity
of his actions. What would make sense of these frac-
tured responses is the conception of "doublethink"
Orwell was to dramatize in *Nineteen Eighty-Four*, the
cementing of simultaneous, contradictory ideas by the
totalitarian impulse. Unfortunately, Koestler is more
interested in the constriction of the political mind, not in
its elasticity.

Any knowledge of Bukharin and his colleagues
adds a historical dimension to this literary difficulty and
makes Koestler seem not only dogmatic but also strangely wilful in his paralyzing of Rubashov's consciousness.

With the exception of the gloomy, short one, the Bolsheviks frequently made ambivalent decisions, choices that involved personal and ideological conflicts. For instance, despite private misgivings and his belief in *cultural* tolerance, Bukharin participated actively in the removal of Trotsky, Zinoviev, and Kamenev, thus allowing Stalin greater control of the Party bureaucracy.[21] In this case, fiction stumbles after biography. Koestler, by insisting on mental gaps and a configuration of psychological fragments, refuses his character such complex yet accessible individuality.

Although we come to understand and accept the confession, we are bound to question how ideological thinking could dominate any man to this extent. We are bound to wonder how, during the Richard and Arlova sequences, Rubashov's logic could be so self-contained as to preclude even a murmuring awareness of alternatives or contradictory feelings. It seems just as puzzling that this man who adores the past should have no memories of the Civil War and his own prominence in the battle for the future. If these issues were left unresolved, *Darkness at Noon* would still be a remarkable exercise in imaginative history. But at the end Koestler does provide an explanation for Rubashov's lack of ambivalence and apparent change.

After the trial Rubashov reflects on his successfully fought temptation to plead for his life, to declare the "subjective" truth and condemn the court itself, "to shout at his accusers like Danton":

> "You have laid hands on my whole life. May it rise and challenge you. . . ." Oh, how well he knew Danton's speech before the Revolutionary Tribunal. He could repeat it word for word. He had as a boy learnt it by heart: "You want to stifle the Republic in blood. How long must the footsteps of freedom be gravestones? Tyranny is afoot; she has torn her veil, she carries her head high, she strides over our dead bodies."

Like most of the Bolshevik intellectuals, Rubashov
was obsessed with the French Revolution, but instead
of the ideologically pure speeches of Robespierre or
Saint-Just's *Republican Institutions*, he memorized
Danton's accusation. As a young revolutionary, Rubashov's mind was not stamped with visions of justice,
with declarations of angry righteousness, but with an
announcement of tyranny, betrayal, and decay. That
the fascination with Danton's trial is more than a high-
lighted detail from the past is clear from another
glimpse of Rubashov's political education.

"As a boy, he had believed that in working for the
Party he would find an answer to all questions [of
human suffering]. The work had lasted forty years, and
right at the start he had forgotten the question for whose
sake he had embarked on it. Now the forty years were
over, and he returned to the boy's original perplexity."
Koestler's bizarre and frightening suggestion is that "the
question" is by nature incompatible with the empirical
world, that it cannot survive even the first moments of
contact with political choice and action.

These memories of his youth are not simply
appropriate to Rubashov's state of mind after the trial;
they account for his behavior, his sensibility, and they
ultimately define the novel's ethical center. In a review
of Koestler's autobiography, Stephen Spender remarks:
"At moments one suspects that [he] thinks that a pattern
of behavior is the same as an existence, just as he
appears to think that the pursuit of a goal is the same as
attaining one."[22] Out of a hidden metaphysic or mere
impatience with intervening and irrelevant detail,
Koestler asks us to believe in *Darkness at Noon* that the
end of the Revolution is not just implicit in the beginning, but is *identical* with it, that vision and terror are
indistinguishable twins. The "premises" of Rubashov's
political career are the same as the conclusions. From
this wholly terrifying, deeply antihistorical perspective,

there is no linear process of change. The difference between Rubashov in the Civil War and Rubashov as a functionary of No. 1 is an illusion that belongs only to the porter, Vassilij. Rubashov need not be aware of doubts or of a more complex political understanding because as Koestler conceives him, Rubashov in the very act of commitment forfeited ordinary selfhood. Mind became ideology.

Inevitably, Koestler's metaphoric language reflects the stasis in Rubashov and in the novel's intellectual framework. Like the ocean, history is profound and disinterested; it absorbs all individual errors and feelings. The masses are its depths, its anonymous well. Other revolutionary parties understood only the surface changes of this vast ocean, but the Bolsheviks succeeded because they "descended into the depths" and "discovered the laws of her inertia." Clearly, the prevalent association of the sea is with the logic of history and the implementation of the Revolution.

But throughout the novel, the sea also symbolizes the contradiction of reason by the more elemental and subjective nature of man. Bogrov's terrible whimpering and the primeval ecstasy of the prisoners' drumming "smothered the thin voice of reason, covered it as the surf covers the gurgling of the drowning." The "silent partner" prompts the perception of infinity that Rubashov describes as the Freudian "oceanic sense." The tension between private and ideological attitudes to life is completely immobilized by these identical images.

The sense of distinct planes of experience—between which Koestler and Rubashov cannot allow any contact—is also produced by the novel's religious motifs. Through Vassilij, the image of the *Pietà*, and Rubashov's stunted vision of a new breed of monks, Koestler creates a firm association of religious feeling and biblical language with the affirmation of the personal. This kind of religion, like the "grammatical fiction," voices a gentle morality and compassion for mankind.

After the trial, Vassilij sees Rubashov as the suffering Christ, but Koestler also identifies Christ with No. 1, the creator of suffering, in order to extend the idea that closed systems like the Bolsheviks' militant philosophy develop a rigid hierarchical structure and become dogmatic: "The old man with the slanting Tartar eyes . . . was revered as God-the-Father, and No. 1 as the Son. . . . From time to time No. 1 reached out for a new victim amongst them. Then they all beat their breasts and repented in chorus of their sins." Rubashov voices Koestler's most fundamental belief at this time—that revolutionary commitment is religious in origin. But by defining both poles of Rubashov's argument with himself, the religious allusions again suggest that public and private faiths are irreconcilable, that historical responsibility and personal conscience are implacable but static enemies.

Decades after the Moscow Trials and Stalinism, the debate over Rubashov's confession has lost some of its intensity, some of its threat to the vestiges of modern man's sense of innocence. Now we are prepared to believe virtually anything about the totalitarian mind. The essential fascination with *Darkness at Noon*, beneath the obvious narrative compulsions, lies in the curious bond between the author and the spirit of the Bolshevik intellectuals. The paradox is not that Koestler sees them as great men and as criminals, but that his judgment of what doomed the Revolution stems from the same quality in him—a corrosive rationalism which paralyzes choice, obliterates ambivalence, and pulls the novel away from history and the greatness of which it was genuinely capable.

# 4

## Therapy, Aesthetics, and the Divine: *Arrival and Departure*

*Arrival and Departure* (1943) was the first novel Koestler wrote in English. A product of his early years of feverish political and social activity among London's wartime intellectuals, it provides the most easily recognizable evidence of his literary self-consciousness. Here Koestler set out to resolve the dilemma of the political novelist not only by means of specific devices such as balanced organization and meticulous patterns of metaphors and parables, but primarily through the choice of what he believed was a special kind of subject for the period. Koestler's most severe criticism of the Marxist novelists of the "Pink Decade" was that they concentrated on the external aspects of political behavior to the exclusion of the psychological sphere, the ambiguities of commitment.[1] These writers never understood, Koestler suggests, that political activity is just as irrational as sexual behavior, that the search for justice grows from personal complexity.

In *Arrival and Departure* he is concerned with the composition of the "political libido," with the hidden springs behind Peter Slavek's revolutionary beliefs, his silence under torture, and his current efforts to enlist in the battle against Hitler. In order to gauge the balance between motive and act, Koestler dramatizes the argument that social values are merely the objectified expression of an individual's psychological needs.[2] This

attitude is reiterated throughout the novel by Sonia
Bolgar who is cast in the dual role of carnivorous hedonist and rigid Freudian:

> Thus, if one wanted to explain why Peter had behaved
> as he did, one had to discard from the beginning his
> so-called convictions and ethical beliefs. They were
> mere pretexts of the mind, phantoms of a more intimate
> reality. It did not matter whether he was a hero of the
> Proletariat or a martyr of the Catholic Church; the real
> clue was this suspect craving for martyrdom.

The manner in which Sonia is proved wrong is the
moral center of the novel. In the ultimate victory of
Peter's new faith and intuition over Sonia's rationalism,
Koestler suggests that man's need for transcendence is
inherent in his being and is capable of a fulfillment
necessary to the age—a position he was to hold until the
tensions of the Cold War years drove him to a desperate
pessimism.

The novel opens with Peter's illegal arrival in "Neutralia" from "somewhere between the Danube and the
Balkans." Twenty-two years old and carrying almost as
many burns, broken teeth, and inner scars, he is no
longer a revolutionary—"the great vision had burnt
itself out"—but still believes in the duty to combat
fascism. While waiting for the British to decide whether
to allow him into their war, Peter lives in Sonia's apart-
ment and for the first time in his life also lives completely in the present. The novelty of the sensual results
in a near rape, then a more restrained love affair with
Odette, a French girl who bears her own stigmata from
the deaths of her fiancé and father.

The day Odette leaves, she asks Peter to join her in
neutral America; on the same day his British visa is
finally granted. The tension between his sense of duty
and the temptation to escape produces a nervous
breakdown and the paralysis of a leg that had been

badly scarred by his country's political police: "It felt as
if all strength had run out of that leg and there was a
queer, numb feeling in the bend of the knee, round the
burn-scar." Through Sonia's "confessional psychology
and dream-surgery," Peter comes to understand that he
had sought in the political world, even in its torture
chambers, atonement for all his childhood guilt, particularly for having wanted to blind his infant brother. The
relentless therapy appears to have illuminated the reality of ethical ideas and acts of heroism: "No more debts
to pay, no more commands to obey. Let the dead bury
their dead. For him, Peter Slavek, the crusade had come
to an end."

But Peter's sense of relief and freedom from the
past is short-lived; something within him refuses to be
satisfied by Sonia's picture of total causation. After he
encounters a disfigured British airman for whom the
issue of motives and reasons is at best peripheral to the
nature of one's actions, Peter dreams that the person he
was before Sonia's treatment, wearing "a rusty coat of
mail," anoints him with an "imaginary cross." And just
before the *Leviathan* sails for America, he receives a
sign in the form of an image from the past, leaves the
ship, and rushes to enlist again in the war against
Germany.

What confused, and then angered, Koestler's readers in wartime England was the mysticism and moral
ambiguity in Peter's rejection of America (identified
with the "subhistorical") and his return to the deluge,
"the rising flood" of totalitarian Europe.[3] Orwell argued:
"The conclusion . . . ought to be . . . that getting rid of
Hitler is still a worth-while objective, a necessary bit of
scavenging in which motives are almost irrelevant."[4]
Indeed, the threat fascism poses to civilization is not
Peter's overriding preoccupation—despite the muted,
eloquent story he told Sonia about the "Mixed Transport" he witnessed, the day-long gassing of "Useless
Jews" who sang as they went to their death.

Nevertheless, the meaning of the war is limited for him, and he echoes Koestler's own sentiment that "we are fighting against a total lie in the name of a half-truth."[5] Peter returns chiefly because he has discovered and accepted a compulsion that stems from a part of his being, an inviolable essence, which the orthodox Freudian cannot reach and explain away. On his "first crusade" he had "set out in ignorance of his reasons; this time he knew them, but understood that reasons do not matter so much. They are the shell around the core; and the core remains untouchable, beyond the reach of cause and effect."

Koestler regards *Arrival and Departure* as "the third novel of a trilogy on ends and means," but in contrast with *The Gladiators* and *Darkness at Noon*, here the problem of expediency is transposed "into terms of individual psychology."[6] What Koestler means by "expediency," however, is Peter's temporary attraction to the prospect of American skyscrapers, libraries, and prolonged showers with Odette. Although these temptations are not genuinely comparable to Spartacus's choice to avoid a massacre of dissidents or Rubashov's decision to sacrifice Arlova, there is one sense in which *Darkness at Noon* and *Arrival and Departure* are complementary. Both novels demonstrate the absolute claims and ultimate inadequacy of what in the autobiography Koestler calls a "closed system." The dominant characteristic of Marxist and Freudian argumentation is that "once you have stepped inside it magic circle," it "deprives your critical faculties of any ground to stand on."[7]

What fascinates Koestler about these "highly developed techniques of casuistry" is the intellectual power that is wielded. In fact, one draws the inference from his memoirs that the dogmatist feels superior and self-assured because he *is* superior. He possesses faith, a state Koestler was inclined—until his later work on psychology—to regard with more admiration than horror.

We see the starkest expression of this reverence in *The Age of Longing* (1951), where a Communist agent is portrayed as the only figure capable of an authentic faith.

But at the time of writing his early novels Koestler felt that it was possible for man to discover an ethically *creative* belief. Given this historical openness, he could temper his respect for the strength Gletkin and Sonia display and represent them as destructive ideologues whose deterministic elimination of the individual can be challenged. The realm of faith that Koestler suggests through Rubashov's "new party" and the "new god" Peter glimpses at the conclusion of *Arrival and Departure* will be the antithesis of these closed systems. Emanating from an intuitive, benign core of self, it will be balanced, cosmic, and, above all, humane.

Yet it is also apparent from these novels that Koestler acknowledges a limited validity in Marxist and Freudian principles. As Harold Rosenberg points out about *Darkness at Noon*, Koestler's "criticism of the Trials . . . accepts the political and historical claims of the Communists while rejecting their moral ones."[8] Koestler's attitude toward analytical explanations is similar. He accepts their accuracy and value for the most obvious levels of motivation: "Behind the achievements of reformers, rebels, explorers, and innovators who keep the world moving, there is always some intimate motivation—and it mostly contains a strong element of frustration, anxiety or guilt."[9]

In *Arrival and Departure* Peter's excessive share of sibling rivalry clearly drove him to find expiation in a revolutionary commitment; Bernard, Sonia's other patient, glorifies the vision of a Fascist "new-born God-state" in order to appease his "nightly attacks of death-fear," his "horror of the void"; and Odette's pouting, wavering sexuality has risen directly from her fiancé's grave. Curiously, the one character who is not diagnostically stamped is Sonia herself, whom Koestler describes through images of primeval monsters and man-eating vegetation, an approach designed to suggest how regressive and inferior her amoral ideology actually is.

In his essays and autobiography Koestler, like most of his contemporaries, insists that in evaluating an artistic or a political expression—a poem about one's mother or a theory of revolutionary insurrection—one must distinguish carefully between motive and act: "The 'reduction' of *social* values like courage and self-sacrifice, to the *psychological* level of masochism, the death instinct, etc., is a process analogous to the reduction of live organisms to their chemical components. For on the sociological level the individual emerges as part of a new whole, and the integrative relations on this level are once more specific and irreducible."[10]

In *Arrival and Departure*, however, the relation of motive to act is far more enigmatic. Because of the concentration of symbols and the emphasis on Peter's new spiritual awareness to the virtual exclusion of the nature of his public actions, Koestler is open to the criticism that he too has reduced human behavior, though to a compartment of the self different from the Freudian's, and in his own terms, has not shown Peter emerging "as part of new whole."

The "old whole" he had been part of, the revolutionary movement we assume to be communism, receives little attention as something possessing an existence in history separate from his neuroses. At the beginning of the novel, Peter is already disillusioned, and at no point does Koestler depict Peter's hopes or the social values he presumably had found in the Party. An even starker imbalance develops in the debate over the Fascists' "biological revolution." Bernard tremulously describes the necessity of genocide, of ethnic "rearrangements" and evolutionary surgery, but Peter's replies to every brutal detail are brief and carry little conviction.

The refutation that contents him is the silent realization that Bernard's philosophy is also rooted in the lush ground of neurosis and private anguish. Peter suddenly recalls Sonia's description of a young man who normally was "active, tense; balanced; but at night he tore his sheets with his teeth and his body shook in rage and despair at the thought of the ultimate inevitability of his death." What leads Peter to this understanding is a physical, not a moral, revulsion from Bernard. His lips become revoltingly moist, "the humidity collecting in the corners and bursting there in tiny bubbles." Koestler allows images of a motive and a mouth to substitute for rational argument or simple horror at the nightmare being drawn over Europe.

One reason for the imbalance in the novel between motive and act emerges in a discussion of Freud that Koestler wrote about the same time. Although Koestler restates his opposition to the "reduction" of complex social behavior to the level of psychological causation, he also makes a curious admission: "*Julius Caesar* has been for ever spoiled for me by the information that the treatment of Brutus by Shakespeare was biased by the trial of Essex; since I read Freud's 'Leonardo' I can't help seeing the Gioconda as a pathological exhibit."[11] Such explanations became fixed in his mind, and he was unable to retain a sense of the whole.

But what also accounts for the treatment of Bernard is the nature of the emotion that German fascism prompted in Koestler. "I found the Brownshirts repellent, but they belonged to a strange and absurd world." The kind of hatred they inspired was "cold . . . without the emotional glow which only intimacy with the hated object can provide." Because "the Nazis were savages who remained true to themselves," Koestler could not respond in the same profound way he could to his own "kin," the prewar Socialists and postwar Communists. "It seems to be a general law in politics that hatred increases in proportion to the amount of shared convictions and interests."[12]

Koestler's selective attitude seems to have altered when the full extent of the Final Solution became known and the question of Palestine arose toward the end of the war. But at the time of writing *Arrival and Departure* Koestler still saw the Nazis as alien, if thoroughly barbaric, creatures, whereas the leftist intellectuals with whom he had shared a humane vision represented the betrayal of history and the great rationalist tradition that had been born in the Enlightenment.

The story of the Mixed Transport that Peter tells Sonia temporarily sharpens the novel's perspective on fascism. First published separately in Cyril Connolly's *Horizon* and based on information Koestler had received from a Polish exile, the episode is one of the most powerful in Koestler's fiction. In its depth of emotion and unselfconscious artistry, the story far surpasses the parables woven into the conclusion of the novel and is comparable only to the Bogrov scene in *Darkness at Noon*. What clearly differentiates the sequence from the rest of the novel is the evenness of tone and the simplicity with which Peter describes the hours of systematic murder:

> The guards sat down on the slope beside the train and rolled cigarettes. The officer remained standing between the two vans, his eyes on the watch in his hand. You could hear nothing but the roaring of the engines of those two immobile vans. This went on for several minutes, and nothing outside seemed to change or to move. There was only the sun, and the rails, and the sky, and the stones. Then a comrade in our carriage said he smelt gas and began to vomit, and several other comrades were sick too; so we shared out our last cigarettes and all smoked.

The description of the locomotive also serves to emphasize the monstrous purpose of the train. Coughing, sparking, whistling, and puffing, the "old-fashioned locomotive" seems to belong to a story for children, not a record of genocide. The incongruity makes its use even more grotesque and horrifying. Because of Koestler's graceful arrangement of details and Peter's almost neutral voice, the inhumanity of the Nazis and the dignity of the old Jews are conveyed with remarkable intensity. The Jews' faith gives them the strength to make their death an exultation in the coming of the Messiah, to behave with gallantry and beauty as on their wedding day, and above all, to show the power of the human spirit over the barbarism that drives these trains: "They are on no time-table, but every night they run in all directions—ten to twenty cattle-trucks locked and bolted, drawn by an old-fashioned locomotive spitting sparks into the night."

The superb narrative control that marks this section does not extend to the entire process of therapy that Peter undergoes. Too often Koestler seems more concerned with demonstrating psychoanalytic theory, with maneuvering handy Freudian notations, than with exploring a fictional character's experiences through the phases of breakdown and recovery. The standard ingredients of analysis are all present: father figures, a variety of trauma, deeply rooted feelings of guilt, transference, dependence on the mother-therapist, and a series of cathartic releases as every layer of the past, each groping for atonement, is revealed.

For Koestler the very choice of this material was a distinct sign of his commitment as a serious novelist. Paradoxically, however, Sonia's inquisition displays the same tendency to oversimplification and contrivance as the Marxist novels Koestler so vehemently condemned. For instance, Sonia finally hints that Peter's relentless search for expiation somehow concerns his younger brother:

> With a jerk Peter sat up, his face flushing hot with anger: "I told you that has nothing to do with it. I didn't do it on purpose."
>
> "Of course not," said Sonia.
>
> "I told you it was an accident. You don't need to look at me that way."
>
> "Tell me, then, how it happened. . . ."
>
> For a last, fleeting moment Peter felt his hostility against Sonia return and surge up in a hot wave of resistance. It was like a rear-guard action of a beaten enemy, though who or what the enemy was he could not say.

Yet the novel escapes being a mere case history grafted on to the repudiation of one philosophy and the affirmation of another, in part because of the richer, if more frightening, images of guilt that hover in Peter's memory of being tortured.

The cruelty of the police and the "almost obscene ecstasy" of Peter's pain suggest a barbarism that predates ideological motives and private neurosis. Torturers and victim share in "the performance of a ritual dance, with the dull inward thunder of his heart and pulses replacing the beating of the sacred drums." This sense of an impersonal, ancient ceremony adheres to another recollection, "dim, lost in the rocking, wavering haze of the cradle—the first scream of frustration and protest, the immaculate conception of guilt." The child's loss of the womb and sharp transition into the world create the initial imprint of guilt and the foundation for subsequent experience.

In Peter's mind the savage dance merges with the memory of birth, and his torturers change their roles. They become "demi-gods in the soft twilight of infancy, dealing out punishment and reward . . . pinioning the wings of early cravings and leaving them forever marked with the snip-scars of anxious guilt." The policemen are the child's parents, establishing limits to his power and completing the destruction of the womb-state. Koestler is, of course, still drawing on his understanding of Freud, but there is nothing mechanical about these sequences. They exhibit, in V. S. Pritchett's terms, Koestler's "terrifying power to describe torture," but their evocative energy also derives from the marriage of the individual and the tribal, the present and the subhistorical.[13] Koestler has added a fundamental dimension to his psychological portrait of an ex-revolutionary. Guilt is not solely the result of a childhood incident, a particular trauma, but is part of the nature of human existence.

In his turmoil after meeting Bernard and the disfigured airman, Peter comes to understand that Adam, not Cain, was the first neurotic, that his guilt has its deepest roots in the human condition. To undo the fall, to erect an artificial innocence, as Sonia demands in her carnivorous primitivism, involves a terrible price. Guilt is fundamental not only to the experience of any child but also to the moral evolution of the species. All human progress, "the prosperity of the race," depends on people who pay "imaginary debts. Tear out the roots of their guilt and nothing will remain but the drifting sand of the desert." If this perception had led directly to Peter's choice of history-bound Europe over the fleshpots of America, it would have been a rational decision having little to do with a mystical future. But since Koestler wants to emphasize the emergence of a new faith, the figure of the guilty Adam retreats behind the novel's proliferating religious metaphors. The figure reappears briefly in the parable of "The Last Judgment" that Peter writes after escaping from the *Leviathan*.

The religious motifs in the novel range in importance from simple analogies to intricate and cooperating symbols designed to register the complexity of motive that Peter accepts at the end. The hold of the ship on which Peter arrived is likened to a cathedral

nave, and the émigré community is compared to a
reverential "flock." Sonia fulfills the role of a "parish
priest" dispensing solace to the members of her congre-
gation. As in *Darkness at Noon*, Koestler is commenting
on the similarity between secular and religious authority, but these limited references seem primarily arranged
for their tonal value, not for their appropriateness to
specific characters. The exiles we meet in the early part
of the novel are, apart from Sonia, neither motivated by
faith nor in search of belief. All they want is safety.

More integral to our sense of character and to the
novel's ultimate perspective is the way Peter describes
the European situation and his part in it. "You have got
out in time," he tells Sonia, "you haven't sat at the waters
of Babylon, weeping." His first betrayal was of a rabbit
named Jerusalem whom he had vowed to keep alive,
and his new commitment is to the "thousand dead in
Zion." It is almost as if Peter never left Sunday school
for classes in Marxist dialectics. Recalling his interrogations, Peter thinks in terms of "the despair of the flesh"
and the battle between flesh and spirit.

Like Rubashov, Peter is briefly pictured as the
suffering Christ. His torturers gloomily ponder "his
crucified body," and the farm laborer who admits he
would have confessed to raping the Holy Virgin falls on
his knees and kisses Peter's hand in reverence. On the
boat that will carry him away from the doomed land,
Peter receives a "sign," accepts the "call" to take his
place in a new priesthood, and embraces "the invisible
cross," which is no longer the emblem of the messianic
revolutionary as we have known him in Koestler's earlier fiction. The faith it epitomizes will be given shape
only by the future, by the arrival of the "global ferment"
Koestler had prophesied and which he translates into
Peter's reborn spirituality.

Just before he returns to his country as an agent,
Peter announces in a letter to Odette: "I think a new god

is about to be born. . . . Praise to the unborn god, Odette." Although he warns her against trying "to divine his message or the form of his cult," Peter is certain that this embryonic divinity will embody the ethical and intuitive qualities of man. His hope is that somehow, parachuting through the night, he is assisting in its birth. What does not touch Peter's consciousness, however, is that he will land in precisely the area of his country where he had watched the "Useless Jews" being gassed. This startling lapse of memory is the ultimate indication in the novel of how personally committed Koestler has become to the "new god," or at least to the moral energy it represents.

Harold Rosenberg finds this near mysticism plain "bafflement," and like Orwell, maintains that the conclusion amounts to an abnegation of critical intelligence.[14] Even if one is less hostile to Koestler's vision, a sense of imbalance is inevitable. At the expense of intellectual and narrative coherence, Koestler feels compelled to express a virtually disembodied hope. It is typical of his fiction that ideas develop an importance distinct from the work itself. What is unusual about *Arrival and Departure* is Koestler's insistence on a morality we cannot fully understand to the exclusion of one rooted in a complex perception of human guilt, a morality central to the richest parts of the novel.

The symmetrical design of the novel is also affected by the imprint of personal belief. Peter's jump from the aircraft is meant to balance his leap from the deck of the *Speranza* at the beginning. His "departure" is also designed as the culmination of the novel's formal development. The movement of each previous section has either been from hope to defeat or from despair to understanding. For example, in Part II, "The Present," Peter exults in the pleasures of the moment, and then Odette leaves. "The Past" begins with Peter's illness and progresses to his ostensibly complete understanding of his motives. By repeating motifs associated with his arrival, torture, love affair, and therapy, "Departure" is arranged to unite all the fluctuations in Peter's experience. As in the other novels, it is an impressive structure, and most of its patterns possess genuine vitality. But the parachute jump is strangely static because we are unable to believe Peter's belief. We cannot follow him to the ground of his country since it is Koestler who has grasped the image of a divinity as yet detached from the world of men. He will hold it like a talisman until history proves its actual worth.

Ultimately, *Arrival and Departure* is of less interest as a coherent, self-contained novel than as an exhibition of Koestler's ethical and artistic beliefs. It is the work that in its most striking techniques best exemplifies the literary theories Koestler held to with little change for over forty years. For instance, he employs a very specific form of obliqueness throughout the novel. Portugal is designated as "Neutralia," the Nazis are usually referred to as "the others," and the English Consulate is unnamed as well; it is "the building with the flag and the heraldic emblem over the gate."

When asked about his insistence on this technique, Koestler replied that one of the most venerable tricks of the artist is the use of the hint.[15] In *The Act of Creation* he calls the device "infolding" and argues that "the intention is not to obscure the message, but to make it more luminous by compelling the recipient to work it out by himself—to re-create it."[16] "Infolding" serves not only the general aesthetic function of making the reader an active "accomplice" but also, one infers, the particular purpose of muting the contemporaneity of the themes Koestler treats.

Unfortunately, the "Neutralia" type of puzzle is simply irritating. It draws attention to Koestler's design without moving the novel toward the ethically universal or engaging the reader's imagination on any funda-

mental level. Koestler is more successful, however,
when the obliqueness defines objects of horror. His
description of "the hated symbol" attains the power and
fascination of the grotesque. "There it spread, with its
scarlet foundation, the thick black ring, and in the middle of it the cross with its broken limbs turned into a
spider." Here the verbal distance, the circumlocution, is
both natural and suggestive; it reflects the revulsion, the
drawing back, one feels from the terror associated with
this emblem.

But the conception of "infolding" is not limited to
specific devices. Koestler maintains that the movement
toward "implicit suggestion" did not begin with the
French Symbolist poets and Impressionist painters, but
rather "is much older, perhaps as old as art itself."[17]
Mythological and biblical archetypes, Plato's dialogues,
and the parables of Christ are all classic forms of
obliqueness. Parables are especially effective in ex-
pressing "the meeting of the trivial narrative of life with
its tragic essence."[18] By an act of imagination, the reader
is lifted above the explicit level of his own experience
on to another, more intense level of perception.

The parables in *The Gladiators*, *Arrival and Departure*, and *Thieves in the Night* all attest to Koestler's
profound concern during that period to keep theory
and practice in general harmony and to be as much of a
"true novelist" as his imagination and moral vision
would allow. In later years he grew increasingly attracted
to the parable form and was perhaps even tempted to
become more of an allegorist than a writer of predominantly realistic narratives. After almost two decades of
work in psychology and the history of science, Koestler
marked his return to fiction with the writing of two
fables, and for the omnibus collection, *Bricks to Babel*,
he selected to represent *Arrival and Departure* only a
brief passage of narrative but both of its parables.[19]

The first of these is a humorous attack on Sonia's

moral reductions. A young man who has been obsessively drawing triangles in the sand tells an oracle, "a solver of riddles," that he wants to discover the secret he believes is hidden in the shape. The "helper of the afflicted" reveals that the youth is subconsciously worried about his wife's faithfulness. With this illumination and the decision to beat her, "the young man, whose name was Pythagoras . . . felt happy and relieved; that dark, inexplicable urge to draw triangles in the sand had left him forever; and thus the Pythagorean Proposition was never found." Koestler explains that the Aegean analyst did not understand that whatever the motives were, the search for the secret of the triangle had an irreducible mathematical integrity.[20]

"The Last Judgment" is a longer, more evocative translation of Koestler's theory into practice. Through a series of haphazard judgments in a dreamlike court, he again suggests that guilt is inevitable and is rooted in the existence of man. Brought to the court past scenes of primeval cruelty, each of the accused, including a crusader remarkably like Peter Slavek, is the guilty Adam and discovers that "he is his own accuser and defender, judge, audience and executioner."[21] Each day the accused go about their ordinary, differentiating tasks, but meet again in the court at night when their common humanity emerges. Paradoxically, the effectiveness of these parables, the imaginative participation they elicit in the reader, makes one even more aware of the religious imposition in the novel's conclusion. The new god neither resolves nor redeems the guilt of birth and moral knowledge.

No interpretive magic can transform Koestler the novelist into Dostoevsky or Koestler the theoretician into Edmund Wilson. But it is a gross oversimplification to assume, as many of his readers do, that Koestler was devoid of a sense of literary tradition and artistic seriousness. As his persistent arguments about the necessity of obliqueness suggest, Koestler, like Orwell and Spender, Malraux and Mailer, was consistently *aware* of the problems inherent in writing political literature. His discussions of fiction and descriptions of the kind of novelist he hoped to become emphasize the moral and intellectual basis of literature and the need to escape the temptations of both propaganda and aestheticism. His favorite metaphor in these essays is the tightrope.

On one side is the morass of literature *enragée* into which most Marxist writing and the equally limited French existentialist novels fell and became petrified.[22] This is the danger of "a boiling-hot vision undigested by the creative process," a manifestation of the "Commissar" mentality.[23] When the intellectual and literary extravagances of the 1930s exhausted themselves, the opposite debasement became dominant. Whereas the radical novelists focused only on their characters' political environment, the "Yogi" writers allow the intricacies of personality to overwhelm all other aspects of experience. The window is shut on the outside world; life is transformed into what Koestler calls the "ultra-violet."[24]

Because he regards the connection between literature and human experience as immediate and inviolable, Koestler can see no value in disembodied flights of creativity. Although in a restricted sense masterpieces, the novels of Proust and Virginia Woolf are inadequate because the unleashed imagination is divorced from a "vision of reality," reality meaning the observable facts of man's life in the world. Although the writer may not wish to use details of our nuclear and totalitarian age directly, his readers must nevertheless be made aware that this world is at least present in his consciousness, that it is shaping his attitudes and perceptions.

Marxist novelists went too far in the right direction, but social writers like Dickens and Zola did not go far enough; they perceived and expressed only fragments of external reality. Koestler's ideal is the balance between art and moral values that Shakespeare and Melville were able to maintain; what he calls *littérature engagée*. *Troilus and Cressida* and *Moby Dick* are in the broadest sense ideological because of their roots in ethical attitudes. But their conceptions of man and society are expressed not in tracts, but in works of art shaped by the writer's traditional sense of himself. "The artist is no leader," Koestler concludes. "His mission is not to solve but to expose, not to preach but to demonstrate. . . . The healing, the teaching and preaching he must leave to others; but by exposing the truth by special means unavailable to them, he creates the emotional urge for healing."[15] An admirable aesthetic thoroughly appropriate to the writer of *The Gladiators* and *Darkness at Noon*, it became increasingly detached from his later work. As Koestler's intense need for faith grew, he was less and less prepared to leave the "healing and preaching" to others.

# 5

## Old Means and a New End: *Thieves in the Night*

In 1946 Koestler published *Thieves in the Night*, a novel about the settlement of a commune in Palestine and the growth of Jewish terrorism as an inevitable response to British policy. The seal between the novel and specific events was extremely tight. In the same year a group of terrorists bombed the King David Hotel in Jerusalem, an event that "marked the beginning of the final phase of British rule in Palestine."[1] Less than a year later, terrorists kidnapped a British judge and in the strange atmosphere of that time talked to him about art and religion and gave him a copy of *Thieves in the Night* to read.[2] What the judge thought of the book was not recorded, but when Israel became a nation, Koestler discovered that the novel had, in fact, played some part in the decisions reached by members of the United Nations Palestine Commission of 1947. This knowledge was, he wrote in retrospect, more gratifying than "the praise and abuse of the literary critics."[3]

All of Koestler's novels were intended to influence the attitudes of his European readers toward certain political issues or events and thereby to have an indirect effect on history. A novel about the Moscow purge trials would, he hoped, help redefine conceptions of the Russian "experiment" and the revolutionary process itself; a novel about an emerging faith might help create "an irresistible global mood." But *Thieves in the Night*

had a more local and immediate goal: to mold public
opinion, especially British opinion, about the urgency
of the Palestine situation and the full scope of the Jews'
claim upon their "National Home" and to depict as
persuasively as possible how the Arab bias in the British
Foreign Office has led to the necessity of terrorism. It is,
then, a work of propaganda, a tactical novel designed
to play a role in a current political controversy. That the
novel largely achieved its public aims is a measure both
of the historical situation and of Koestler's ability to
create a vivid and compelling framework for his
arrangement of ethical positions.

*Thieves in the Night* is a "topical" work, and we are
accustomed to assuming that literature which is directed
at a particular dilemma or moment in history cannot
endure such restrictiveness, cannot be "universal." But
time has conspired with narrative skill to give Koestler's
novel a continuing value. It has survived not because
there have been three wars in the Middle East since
1948, but because violence and terror, which Koestler
felt compelled to support as temporary necessities,
have become almost as intrinsic to our world as those
great personal conflicts some have tried to make the
only worthy and permanent subjects of art.

With the British election of 1945, Koestler had good
reason to anticipate a more humane approach to Palestine. The Labour Party had repeatedly declared its
unequivocal opposition to Chamberlain's White Paper
of 1939 that severely restricted Jewish immigration. But
once in power Labour buried its commitments and
succeeded only in perpetuating the misery of the
"human debris" left over from the Holocaust. In order
to exhibit the wretched lineage of Foreign Office policy
and justify Jewish extremism, Koestler removed his
narrative to the prewar years (1937-39), when it was still
possible to deny Hitler the objects of his Final Solution.

Koestler chose to support terrorism at what he

describes as considerable personal cost: "Of the various crusades in which I had been engaged this was the most harrowing and painful, a penance for the political vagaries of the past. . . . The all-pervading savagery and hatred were active fuel for my anxiety-neurosis, and for a while alcohol was the only remedy."[4] Paradoxically, *Thieves in the Night* is Koestler's most relaxed novel, having none of the ideological solipsism that marks *Darkness at Noon* and *The Age of Longing.* In its diversity of viewpoint and immediacy of visual detail, the novel possesses a breadth that is uncharacteristic not only of Koestler's work but of political fiction in general.

Our perspective on the ethical complexity of Palestine and the growth of Ezra's Tower, the new Jewish commune, comes from a variety of sources: the settlers themselves, the Arabs whom Koestler portrays with skill and sympathy, the American journalist, Matthews, the English officials who play out Koestler's notions about public-school repression, and the terrorists who submit to the logic of the moral "ice age." To accentuate the documentary element of the narrative, Koestler makes liberal use of quotations from Hansard and the Book of Ezra and inserts italicized editorial descriptions of the political controversy over Jewish immigration to Palestine. Usually these points of view evolve from, or return to, the novel's center: the attitude toward the commune, ghetto Jews, and the problem of violence expressed in diaries by Joseph, a half-Jewish settler from England. Joseph's transition from cobbler to underground propagandist commands much of Koestler's attention—for most readers an unworthy and distracting preoccupation in what is otherwise a vital, if morally disquieting, narrative.

In the opening section, "The First Day (1937)," the settlers, each with a "thing to forget" from Europe's "night of the long knives," hope to find in the building of the commune a home and a return to normality. They erect a watchtower and the rudiments of buildings, debate the issue of terrorism, and beat off the first night attack by the neighboring Arabs. After the battle, Joseph reflects that Jews "are the exposed nerve, an extreme condition of life," that "to be approved of, to like and to be liked" is true bliss. Approval is neither Dina's goal nor instinct. In the tranquillity of the night she is able to lie with her head on Joseph's arm, a remarkable moment for her since usually "she could not bear to be touched," a legacy of revulsion from her German interrogators. "Sleep, Dina," Joseph tells her, "you are safe; we are both safe here."

In "More Days (1938)" Joseph chronicles the growth and daily life of the commune: the marriages, child-rearing, financial maneuverings, the rain and mud, and inspections from the British secretariat. Colliding with the lush privacy of the commune is the news that the respected Bauman has deserted his social democratic origins and has joined "Jabotinsky's right-wing extremists." Joseph is not yet prepared for an irrevocable commitment to the new demands of survival and accepts a weekend marriage with a girl he treats as a poor substitute for the still withdrawn and anguished Dina.

"Days of Wrath (1939)" brings Joseph and his brethren closer to the issuing of the White Paper and the stoking of the furnaces. With every hour the argument for violence becomes more self-evident and irrefutable. Joseph watches the immigrant boat, the *Assimi*, being turned back to Central Europe, and while discussing Zionism with Matthews, he discovers that Dina has been raped and murdered. Revenge for her death is taken by the terrorists against the head of the Arab village, and Joseph is finally allowed to visit Bauman who discourses on the primacy of survival—that violence is "a global infection against which the only

defence was to get contaminated oneself." They
encounter a rabbinical student who is carrying a small-
arms manual in the traditional prayer bag of the
Orthodox Jew; he chants the details of the gun's mecha-
nism as he would intone a prayer to the Name. Joseph's
conversion is less mystical. He is allowed to remain at
Ezra's Tower where he writes propaganda releases for
Bauman's group.

"The Day of Visitation (1939)" details the massive
demonstrations that were mounted in Jerusalem against
Chamberlain's formal strangling of immigration and
the sale of Palestinian land to Jews. "Thieves in the
Night (1939)" concludes the narrative with the establishment of a new commune by settlers with an even
heavier load of "things to forget." Joseph reflects on the
uniqueness of Jewish nationalism: "It is the return from
delirium to normality and its limitations. . . . We have
occupied another acre of space. The hunt will go on and
the stakes will keep burning, but a few hundred will live
here; and the wilderness shall be glad for them."

What did not gladden Koestler's readers was the
"extraordinary contradiction between *Darkness at Noon*
and *Thieves in the Night*."[5] Just before his execution,
Rubashov haltingly decides that the precept by which
"he had sacrificed others and was himself being sacrificed"—that the end justifies the means—is horribly
wrong. However, a (fictional) year later in Palestine,
Bauman and Joseph accept the necessity of "violent and
detestable means." The immigrants deported to the
gates of the concentration camps, the wailing of sirens
as the ships are turned back from safety in Palestine,
make "all moral scruples" irrelevant. Koestler did not
evade the issue of the different mood and ethical conception of *Thieves in the Night*. Its "central theme," he
says, "is the ethics of survival. If power corrupts, the
reverse is also true: persecution corrupts the victim,
though perhaps in subtler and more tragic ways."[6]

Koestler's first novels and essays show him exploring the dilemma of revolutionary ethics in a context of absolute choice and judgment. But with the end of the war and a growing awareness of the fate of Europe's Jews, he began to approach questions of political morality on a more pragmatic, relative scale. In an essay, "The Challenge of Our Time" (1947), Koestler argues that the conflict between morality and the logic of expediency "admits no final solution. But each period has to attempt a temporary solution adapted to its own condition. . . . Without the rebellion of the Barons, there would be no Magna Carta; without the storming of the Bastille, no proclamation of the Rights of Man."[7] He goes on to insist, though, that the consequences of major political surgery are "unpredictable," "that the End only justifies the Means within very narrow limits."[8]

For Koestler these limits were geographical and ideological. Although the "political ice age," as Bauman calls his era, existed everywhere after the war, Europe and Palestine remained, largely out of personal need, sharply differentiated in Koestler's mind. In an earlier essay about the plight of Europe, he counseled his "fraternity of short-term pessimists" not to "brandish the surgeon's knife at the social body, because they know that their own instruments are polluted."[9] When they act, like Peter in *Arrival and Departure*, it will be with the assurance that they are somehow drawing closer the blessed emergence of "a spiritual spring-tide like early Christianity or the Renaissance."[10]

If general moral contamination should restrain extreme political action in Europe, it meant the complete opposite in Palestine. In 1945 Zionism did not represent a new god or spiritual awakening. For Koestler it was the agony of an oppressed, if disagreeable, people whose needs had been horribly defined by the Nazi bureaucracy:

During their two thousand years of exile, never have

more Jews been murdered than in the two years from
1942 to 1944; never have they been more in need of a
national haven. They were denied it by men otherwise
kind and well-meaning, who had become victims of a
strange obsession, a mirage of the desert.[11]

The postwar situation in Palestine demanded relative
judgments and a pragmatic morality. Because the survival of the refugees from Europe and the Jews in the
Middle East meant nationhood, not political revolution,
violence could be limited and decisive without involv-
ing questions of ideology or vast currents of historical
change.

If these arguments alone—what Isaac Rosenfeld
called "the natural justification of violence"—had
shaped the themes of the novel, the sense of betrayal
and revulsion that readers experienced might not have
been so acute.[12] But somehow, perhaps through the
process of writing, perhaps the real as well as the fictional company in Jerusalem of the "violent people, the
people with grenades in their lorries," what entered the
novel was a frighteningly easy subordination of means
to ends.[13] The turmoil Koestler felt in supporting terrorism was no doubt genuine, but it too was transformed
into a ready, almost a welcome, submission to necessity.[14]
restraint, ethics and the purity of the cause." At the end
of the novel, Joseph does not merely accept the dark,
"good conscience" in the political man), Simeon, a
character who is drawn with unqualified sympathy,
contemptuously dismisses "the whole menu" of "self-
restraint, ethics and the purity of the cause." At the end
of the novel, Joseph does not merely accept the dark,
moral imperative of violent retaliation; he becomes
quite eloquent in his praise for the "political imagina-
tiveness" and "submission to discipline" found only
"among extremist movements of the tyrannical type."
The language, the tone, Koestler permits himself in
these passages is an appalling if implicit repudiation of

his earlier work, particularly *Darkness at Noon,* and of
the growth of his political understanding in pain and
compassion.

Although Joseph becomes one of "the violent people," he remains the most mundane of Koestler's pro-
tagonists. One can find virtually no resemblance
between his fondness for homey philosophizing and
Rubashov's awesome meditations, or between his usually congenial presence and the enigmatic power of
Spartacus. Joseph represents, in fact, a further reduction of commitment that had begun with Peter Slavek.
Koestler's design is clear, though. The more ordinary
the protagonist, the more unavoidable and convincing
the need for extreme action will appear. Unlike Simeon
and Bauman, Joseph's Zionism was not defined by the
knowledge of which of his relatives had been sent to
Belsen, which to Auschwitz. Joseph's memories are of
ponies, an English country home, and a Jewish father he
comes to revere, first through an "incident" with a lady
Fascist, then a commitment to Palestine.

Joseph and Simeon adopt a credo that concen-
trates the central ideas in the novel: "This was the hour
of the deed, and not of its malicious inward echo. The
world will know only about the deed—the echo shall be
effaced." For the good of a potential nation, one must
forgo the luxury of conscience and even the understanding of one's drives and motives. Whereas Koestler
is far more prepared in this novel to distinguish
between motive and act, the belief that political choices
arise from trauma and guilt continues to dominate his
approach to character. With the larger cast of *Thieves
in the Night,* the quality of diagnosis ranges considera-
bly. It is typical of Joseph's uncertain value as a major
figure that his "Incident" is the most misconceived episode in the novel.

While home from Oxford, Joseph has his first sexual experience, with a woman who supports Mosley's

Fascists. "But Joseph at that time was not interested in politics." He is, however, quickly on the emotional route to Palestine when, after they make love, the light "revealed their nudity, and with it the sign of the Covenant on his body, the stigma of the race incised into his flesh." The woman becomes distraught, and Joseph subsequently begins to atone for his part in the "conspiracy of silence" that had grown around his dead Jewish pianist father. In a recent postscript to the novel, Koestler apologized for not knowing that circumcision was a hygienic as well as a religious practice in England.

Apart from his treatment of Joseph, Koestler's approach to the private echoes of the other chief characters is controlled and powerful. There is nothing stereotyped and vulgar about the picture of Dina "sitting alone in the empty Children's House," or the silent presence of Simeon's sister every time he plants a sapling. Their memories prompt our compassion and our understanding that "the world of yesterday" is poised to submit to the present. Joseph's phrase, "the echo shall be effaced," symbolizes the impetus of the novel and the potentiality within Palestine itself. In this novel the bond between emotions and political action is remarkably simple; traumas are the accidents of history and the triggers for choices which, nevertheless, have a separate, irreducible value. Here Koestler does not dwell on the mystery of one's hidden being, but rather upon the uncluttered duty and compulsion to survive.

One ingredient in Koestler's Zionism, a "malicious, inward echo" of his own, was his loathing for the language, physical qualities, and "ghetto mentality" of European Jews. A Jewish state would, he believed, eradicate these flaws "which seemed intimately connected with the Jews' lack of a country and a flag of their own."[15] In the novel these attitudes are transferred to Joseph. Because he is in part an outsider, Joseph's appraisal of Jews and Jewishness is meant to be particularly effective. But there is nothing objective in his feeling "that he was surrounded by masks of archaic reptiles. . . . It was no good denying to himself that he disliked them, and that he hated even more the streak of the over-ripe race in himself." In small doses Joseph's revulsion from the ugliness, the humid "knowingness," of the ghetto-bred immigrants could have intensified his value as a spokesman for extreme nationalism. But his frequent expressions of disgust tend to diminish his more benign assertions about the land and the urgency of the pressures on the settlers. Joseph's summary of his politics is especially grotesque: "I became a socialist because I hated the poor; and I became a Hebrew because I hated the Yid."

By dwelling on this contempt, Koestler at one point in particular displays a startling insensitivity to the process of the narrative he has created. Surveying the Jews in a Tel Aviv restaurant, Joseph tells Matthews that the ghetto has prevented the development of "tradition, form, style," that the Dead Sea is "the perfect symbol" for the race: "over-salted, over-spiced, saturated." Not only are these remarks ill-considered, they are also ill-timed since they occur immediately after a scene that ends with the attack on Dina by Arab villagers—a brutal, unsettling episode which by itself virtually persuades us that militancy is the Jews' only recourse in Palestine. Although Joseph's assaults on ghetto culture are not directed at Dina, their generalized, confused expression of disgust inadvertently trivializes her death and distances the reader from a comprehensible and human justification of violence.

The characters of Dina and Simeon, in fact the entire rendering of life at Ezra's Tower, exist at one level of the novel, whereas Joseph's theories exist on another. He finds the cause of centuries of persecution in the very nature of the Jews: "With all the boons we have brought to humanity we are not liked, and I suspect the reason is that we are not likable." The inability to be liked is equated with homelessness, and the only "cure" is the security of a sovereign state. Founded on the values of social approval and manners, it is certainly an original conception of nationalism. But when Dina was tortured in Germany, it was because she was a woman with a politically important father, not because she was unlikable. Simeon and Bauman came from less distinguished families, but again because of race and politics, they found themselves hounded and without a home. Indeed, none of the builders of Ezra's Tower conforms to Joseph's stereotype of personality or reptilian appearance.

When freed of the grip of racial obsession, *Thieves in the Night*—whether one wants to call it "a genuine novel" or "a series of dispatches"—is an authentic, comprehensive view of the Jewish settlement and surrounding Palestinian life.[16] "In no other novel does Koestler devote so much space to conveying the quality of the life of his characters."[17] In its precision of detail, it is close to the texture of *The Gladiators*. But where the reader's perception of the Roman world depends upon both emotional and historical distance, the perspective on Ezra's Tower requires a simple, direct understanding of the intensely personal investment the settlers have made in the land.

As they approach the hill for the first time, Joseph explains: "When a Jew returns to this land and sees a stone and says, This stone is mine, then something snaps in him which has been tense for two thousand years." The hills of Galilee are shaped like a woman's body, and Dina can imagine that the growth of the fields will echo in the birth of her own children. As the details of routine life at Ezra's Tower accumulate—the claiming of the land, the raising of the animals and crops—we become increasingly aware that a normal existence is at least within the grasp of the settlers. Although Koestler does not always seem to realize it, their right to the ordinary is the novel's most compelling argument for Jewish nationalism.

Despite the novel's clear political bias, Koestler endows his portrayal of the Arabs' way of life with equal authenticity. A long section is devoted to the peacemaking ceremony between the rival clans of the village. Although a Bedouin guest calls it a mockery staged for the benefit of the English, the strained meeting of the old leaders is highly dramatic and effectively suggests the ceremonial framework of Arab society. Koestler emphasizes the decay of this tribal structure in the modern world and conveys a genuine sense of regret at such inevitability. He also depicts the pathos of Arab traditionalism through the boundaries of the Mukhtar's own consciousness.

The village leader presented Koestler with essentially the same kind of artistic problem he faced with the Roman slaves in *The Gladiators*. To capture what were alien mentalities, Koestler was forced beyond the translation of his own experience and "typicality" into distinctive leaps of imagination. The Mukhtar is taken to the same place where Dina was murdered and comes to understand the reason for his death when it is explained in the terms of his world: "The Mukhtar dimly realised that the Yemenite was talking sense. . . . The world around him grew confused, he was back in the days of his youth, haggling with Bedouins over a blood feud. . . . He began to recite like a litany the traditional list of camels to be paid." Koestler allows the Arab a sad dignity and at the same time indicates the nature of the larger struggle. The Mukhtar's life is to be a token installment; Dina and the other refugees will not be repaid by camels or blood, only by nationhood.

Koestler is particularly sympathetic to the Arabs in their love for the age-old appearance of the hills and land surrounding their villages. When the Mukhtar's father is informed about the arrival of the Jews and their construction of the first buildings, "he stood erect and motionless at the parapet," his blind eyes "lifted to the hills." The very idea of the settlement disrupts a chain of memory that has extended over the centuries from his ancestors to him. His silent grief marks the essential difference between the Arabs' bond with the land as their God created it and the attitude of the Jews for whom the land provides the raw material of their own creativity. But there are sharp limits to Koestler's sympathy for the Arabs. When their traditionalism feeds on cruelty, he becomes again the consummate propagandist for Zionism. Despite the Mukhtar's great wealth, the village children's "eyes were sticky with the Egyptian disease and flies were crawling over them in clusters." The Mukhtar says that it is God's will, a complacency which horrifies the author and his characters. The Jews will bring both medicine and a greater sense of compassion to Palestinian life.

Between the perspectives of the settlers and the Arabs, Koestler steadily builds up a striking visual quality to the novel. In fact, the centrality of the landscape and the contrasting cities makes *Thieves in the Night* unique among Koestler's novels. By comparison, the rest of his fiction, with the exception of *The Gladiators*, is intensely claustrophobic. A sense of confinement is, of course, artistically integral to *Darkness at Noon* because the imprisoned mind of Koestler's aging, guilty Bolshevik is the subject, indeed the novel itself. But in *Arrival and Departure* and *The Age of Longing* the details of the physical environment, the cafés, the streets, even the appearance of people, exist solely within the boundaries of the novel's developing ethical structure. Only when the narrative moves to particular incidents in the past, such as the story of the Mixed Transport, does this sense of confinement temporarily lift.

*Thieves in the Night* embodies Koestler's implicit acknowledgment that a world exists, even if tentatively, outside the political intellect. His background in the Middle East is significant here. In the autobiography Koestler recounts how in 1926 he wandered through Palestine as a young vagabond with little concern for political questions. Then, through an Austrian painter in Cairo, he learned "to see, without thinking, in purely visual terms, and to perceive human beings— some sailors on the Nile or a beggar on the steps of a mosque—as incidental figures in a timeless landscape."[18] It was also a landscape from which Koestler could maintain a fundamental distance, even in 1945. Despite his anxieties about advocating violence and his passionate concern for the refugees from the Holocaust, Palestine did not engage him at his most profound level of commitment—which was always ideological. Koestler made the difference between his commitments very clear when he told an American reporter: "The Russian danger is so urgent that I wouldn't hesitate to sacrifice the Palestine issue to this larger issue if I were convinced that a Jewish Palestine would strengthen the Russian position."[19] Because it deals with a "smaller" issue, the novel is allowed to develop a sense of objective space and moral independence.

The landscape is also important in terms of the novel's language. Throughout Koestler's fiction the main source of his imagery is the Old Testament, but in the land of Moses and the Prophets religious metaphors and biblical rhythms have an unusual and natural legitimacy. There is, however, an essential difference between the function of this language in *Thieves in the Night* and its role in the other novels. Rubashov, Spartacus, Nikitin in *The Age of Longing*, even the early Peter Slavek, are driven by a messianic quest for social justice. In keeping with the limitations of Koestler's renewed Zionism, no character in this novel embodies the messianic instinct. Bauman explains: "When they locked me up I had time to think it over and decided that the moment had come for us to stop redeeming the world, and to start redeeming ourselves. We can't wait until socialism solves all racial problems." In *Arrival and Departure* "Jerusalem" is a metaphor for a revolutionary commitment; for Koestler's Zionists it is a tangible goal in a clash of nationalisms.

Ever since the Dispersion, Joseph realizes, the survival of the Jews has depended upon their adherence to religious symbols. Even now belief in the efficacy of symbols persists. The Orthodox Jews in Palestine anticipate the intervention of God, and the "reasonable" settlers regard the communes as a powerful political emblem. But the novel sanctions Bauman's argument that in the present crisis symbols which bind an army are what is required for the race to endure. The Bible, menorah, and revolver are Bauman's "paraphernalia of nationalism." In the initiation ceremony that Joseph witnesses, the soldier's "wide-open eyes were fixed for a second or two on the flame of the candles, skirted the Bible and stuck fascinatedly on the revolver." Neither Koestler nor his spokesmen seem particularly troubled by the transformation of historical ritual into ecumenical expediency.

This lack of discomfort is reflected in the easy, rambling quality of the narrative method itself. Again contrasting with the sense of stasis in most of the other novels, *Thieves in the Night* is always in motion, which is entirely appropriate to a situation in which political action rather than intellect plays the major role. There is virtually none of the self-conscious, intricate weaving of characters and events typical of *Darkness at Noon* and *The Age of Longing*. Here the structure is open and simple. Even Koestler's passion for balance, what Clement Greenberg calls his "contrapuntal effects," has a different quality that stems from his unusual wariness

of rigid impositions.[20] The opposing views of the landscape, for instance, are not editorial constructions, but
are thoroughly intrinsic to the lived experience of the
major figures.

Like Koestler's other endings, the conclusion of
*Thieves in the Night* is symmetrical; the settlers who
founded Ezra's Tower are now preparing to assist in the
creation of another commune. Details are repeated
from the opening of the novel: the newcomers are
referred to as "debutants," and an identical speech is
given by one of the patriarchs of the settlements. Joseph
lies on top of a truck as before, but at this point the tone
we have come to expect from Koestler's symmetrical
patterns alters totally. In the other novels, even in *Arrival and Departure*, the sense of spatial limitation is
intensified by the enclosed quality, the inwardness,
created by the final repetitions. *Thieves in the Night*,
however, opens toward an uncertain, though very real
and hopeful future. No doubt Koestler's original plan to
have the novel carry on to the end of the war and "the
peaceful growth of Ezra's Tower" helped this openness
develop.[21]

But in retrospect, one is inclined to see in the unselfconscious ending the separation of the novelist from the
future of his characters. Koestler explains in his historical account of Palestine, *Promise and Fulfilment* (1949):

> These conclusions [that Jews should move to Israel or
> assimilate to their particular culture], reached by one
> who has been a supporter of the Zionist Movement for a
> quarter-century, while his cultural allegiance belonged
> to Western Europe, are mainly addressed to the many
> others in a similar situation. They have done what they
> could to help to secure a haven for the homeless in the
> teeth of prejudice, violence and political treachery.
> Now that the State of Israel is firmly established, they
> are at last free to do what they could not do before: to
> wish it good luck and go their own way, with an occa-

sional friendly glance back and a helpful gesture. But, nevertheless, to go their own way, with the nation whose life and culture they share, without reservations or split loyalties.[22]

He was only temporarily sharing the settlers' aspirations. They move toward a nation; Koestler, his political integrity more or less intact, returned to an anguished Europe and the grim allegiances of *The Age of Longing*.

# 6

## The Pathology of Faith:
## *The Age of Longing* and *Twilight Bar*

Whatever their individual merits or flaws, the novels considered thus far all possess an undeniable vitality. In these works Koestler lays just claim upon the reader's admiration for the imaginative shape he makes of history and political ideas. These novels communicate Koestler's sense of artistic integrity, his voice of moral urgency, and his confidence in himself as a witness and recorder of the momentous events of our time. But with *The Age of Longing* (1951), the last piece of fiction Koestler was to complete for seventeen years, intellectual vigor and literary control fall away. What remains is Koestler's contempt for Europe's spiritual emptiness and the loss of its will to withstand the Soviet state, represented in the novel by the "Commonwealth of Freedomloving People" and its agent, Nikitin, whom Koestler pointedly makes a friend of Gletkin's, the brutal interrogator in *Darkness at Noon*.

In a recently written preface, Koestler emphasized the need to understand "the political situation in Europe in the late nineteen-forties which forms the novel's background. . . . It was the world of *Nineteen Eighty-Four* and the period in which it was written."[1] The details he enumerates are a catalogue of political horrors: the intensity of the Cold War, Stalin's "reign of terror," the Berlin blockade, the Communist *coups* in Eastern Europe, the World Peace Movement, and the

part played in it by left-wing intellectuals.[2] Because of
the strength of the French Communist Party and the
dangerous self-deception of the country's most influential thinkers—particularly those, we recall, who personally declined to accept Koestler's prophecies—he
set the novel in Paris and only a few years in the future.
"It merely carries the present one step further in time—
to the middle nineteen-fifties."[3]

Like most of his contemporaries, Koestler never
found it easy to reconcile art and politics, but the task
became insurmountable or simply trivial compared
with his need to punish actual individuals and an entire
culture, to settle accounts with himself and the future.
Julien, who voices many of Koestler's central ideas in
the novel, says that "a single look from Nikitin's eyes"
makes his imagination "wish to retire to a nunnery or to
preach a sermon—and when a writer becomes a
preacher, he is finished." Julien chooses to stop writing
poetry; Koestler's choice was to relinquish contemplation and objectivity, to erode the boundaries between
the political essay and political novel, and with full
awareness of the artistic consequences, to preach ser-
mons on the need for unshakable, unquestioning belief.

This need is embodied in the relationship between
Nikitin and Hydie, an American ex-Catholic whose
father is in Paris drawing up a list of Frenchmen to be
the "nucleus of the future liberation army and liberation
government." They meet at a party Monsieur Anatole
holds to celebrate the anniversary of the French Revolution, but the gathering is more like a wake for French
"continuity," because now, like the rest of Europe,
France is doomed, diseased, threatened with "the
advent of Neanderthal." Hydie represents this weakness in individual terms. She sees herself as having "no
core, no faith, no fixed values. How right that Russian
had been to look at her with such disgust."

In consecutive chapters Koestler draws a number

of comparisons between the backgrounds of Nikitin and Hydie and the process of change their beliefs underwent. The memory of her alcoholic mother fills Hydie with loathing, and she recalls that the day after her mother left the family for good, she experienced her first menstruation. As "the unclean daughter of an unclean mother," Hydie welcomed the purity of the convent. But her conception of Christianity was inevitably transformed from a simple vision of divine compassion and love to a recognition of the need for dogma. "Her faith . . . developed a rigid, elaborate frame and structure" that led her to a "true" understanding of "the enemy camp" and the value of the Inquisition.

The immediate source of Nikitin's faith is a parent as well. But Nikitin's legacy is not a desire to escape, to purge himself of uncleanliness. His father, Grisha, has left him something more durable and powerful: "a message of hatred, cruelty and revenge; it was also a message of love, of unshakable faith in the Great Change." The story of Nikitin's family reflects the same movement from compassion to dogma and intolerance that Hydie experienced in her faith. Like Hydie's initial understanding of Christ, the politics to which Nikitin's grandfather, Arin, clings are humane and morally pure. But Grisha reluctantly accepts the necessity of harsh methods, and Nikitin completes the transition to the rigidity and abstractness of modern ideology. He easily learns that the progress of the Revolution is more important than conscience, that the past and the people's enemies must be conquered. In these sections Koestler is explicitly demonstrating that faith becomes inhumanly systematized and that communism is a stronger, more compelling ideology for the modern world than its closest rival, Catholicism.

Koestler's thinly disguised caricatures of real individuals are concentrated during the "Witches' Sabbath," a "Rally for Peace and Progress" that Hydie

attends with Julien. Koestler's point about all the famous intellectuals praising the Free Commonwealth is
that they are "bewitched," but believe that their ideas
have a rational foundation. When an official change in
Commonwealth policy becomes evident through a
speech given by Hero of Culture Leontiev, the intellectuals determine, with the ease that comes from constant
self-deception, to accommodate their arguments in
whatever way necessary or possible.

To confirm again the amoral power in Nikitin's
selfless devotion, the narrative shifts to the early years
of the Revolution in Moscow and to his sense of living
"in the first day of creation, when the heaven and the
earth were being divided out of the chaos." Like
Koestler himself, Nikitin betrays a woman, also named
Nadeshda, who "displayed an attitude of frivolousness
towards our task of socialist reconstruction." But Nikitin never thinks about her again, and the only effect the
denunciation has on him is thoroughly gratifying. It
initiates his career with the State Security force, the
culmination of which is his role in Paris as a planner for
future executions. Leontiev, on the other hand, ends his
career in Paris when he defends the "Fearless Sufferers"
publicly. Although small in number, the members of
this religious sect pose a threat to the Commonwealth
because they, like their enemies, act "in sincere faith."

Between Parts One and Two of the novel is an
"Interlude" that begins with a nuclear explosion which
destroys a town in the Free Commonwealth. Wielding
the weapons of Socialist Sarcasm, the Father of the
People persuades the world that it was an American
device dropped by a hostile power. The Americans
fumble defensively, the guilty "Rabbit Republic" is
overthrown, Europe is grateful for the restraint shown
by the Free Commonwealth, disease from the fallout
spreads, and Frenchmen take to wearing Geiger-counter
watches and fashionable anti-radiation umbrellas.

In Part II, one of Julien's friends, Professor Vardi, decides to return to the Commonwealth. Tired of being an exile and a victim, he is prepared to submit to its dedication, its "absolute unquestioning faith" in the future. It is "like feeling all of a sudden young again." Later, after Vardi's trial for espionage opens in Viennograd, Julien calls a meeting of leading writers to discuss "the possibility of organised intellectual resistance under the regime" that will soon occupy France. A complete failure, the "meeting had turned out more or less as expected: he had done what he could, and procured an alibi before his conscience."

Leontiev's alibi comes from a bottle and the noisy company of other émigrés. His inability to write about his life as a "hero of culture" becomes increasingly calcified, and he takes a job reading Russian poetry at a nightclub. Years of acquiescence in abhorrent policies have completely eroded his will, and the mere presence of Nikitin at the club forces Leontiev to set up and accept his own extradition. "It seemed to him that he had always known it would end in this way." Then Nikitin sets out to prove that there are no great psychological mysteries, only reflexes, by experimenting on Hydie's body. Besides being sexually degrading, the experience ties Hydie again to the isolation of the body, for which she cannot forgive Nikitin.

Hydie is unable to convince the French authorities that they should arrest Nikitin for compiling elimination lists of notable intellectuals, but Commanche, a Resistance hero, tells her that "each time a god dies there is trouble in History," that Nikitin cannot be overcome until Europe has "a new, more up-to-date" god. All Hydie can supply is a pistol with which she tries, and fails, to kill Nikitin. Her sense of certainty, the "radiant stillness" that came from her decision to rouse the public by "a symbolic act of protest," collapses into "bottomless" despair. Nikitin, however, almost welcomes a

scandal that would send him to a camp in the Arctic.
"She had proved his unworthiness, his vulnerability to
temptation—and at the same time she had shown him
how trite and stale those temptations were." He fears
neither punishment nor death, because only the future
has importance.

At Monsieur Anatole's funeral the future of Europe
seems even closer than usual. There are rumors of para-
chutists in the Rhône Valley, some of the mourners are
planning their escape, and the funeral cortège proceeds
past the great monuments of Paris as though for the last
time. Hydie and her father are returning to America,
while the former leaders of the French Resistance discuss arms caches and strategies for guerrilla warfare.
The will, the capacity to endure, will eventually be
provided by a new faith. Julien quotes Koestler's
"hunch that the time is not far when a new spiritual
ferment will arise, as spontaneous and irresistible as
early Christianity or the Renaissance." Until then Europe
remains "sick with longing." God's place in man "had
become vacant, and there was a draught blowing
through the world."

Koestler has said that the novel is perhaps "over-
structured," but the problem is that the elaborate structure remains devoid of essential humanity.[4] Virtually all
life in the novel suffocates under Koestler's vision of the
rot at the core of European civilization. The general
shape of *The Age of Longing* is much like that of the
other novels; the opening and closing balance one
another with some fundamental thematic variations. At
Monsieur Anatole's Bastille Day party Hydie and her
father watch a rocket shoot into the sky "like a golden
comet." The fireworks which were going to spell out
"the creed of the French revolution" are smothered by a
rainstorm. At the end, the Parisians anxiously ponder
the mysterious and ominous clouds forming in the sky.
"Thus, Hydie thought, must mediaeval crowds have

stared at the sky Anno Domini 999, waiting for the Comet to appear." The conclusion wearily repeats what is apparent from the beginning, that the Rights of Man and the precious living tradition that France embodied are doomed to extinction.

More intricate than this overall pattern is Koestler's compositional approach throughout the novel. Using Hydie as a link, he consistently shifts the focus of the narrative from one side of the spiritual war to the other. Hydie's relationship with Nikitin is balanced and compared with her place among Julien's friends as one of the "dispossessed of faith." The marked contrast of their futile intellectuality with Nikitin's emotional power incessantly proclaims his victory in Koestler's ideological race.

Equally meticulous is another kind of balance maintained throughout: the extension of an action or motif dominant in one chapter into subsequent sections. For instance, after Julien and Vardi have discussed what it means to be a political apostate, Koestler depicts Leontiev in the process of becoming one and the pitiful consequences of his action. Similarly, Leontiev's decision to remain in Paris is followed by Vardi's return to the Free Commonwealth. Both men's great hopes for their freedom are rapidly demolished. As in *Darkness at Noon*, this weaving of connections between characters is a thematic technique, but here it remains starkly detached from personality or mind. Like a prosecutor, Koestler is amassing a quantity of evidence to prove the futility of any action that does not have its origins in absolute belief.

There is, however, one part of the structure that has genuine vitality. When Koestler describes Nikitin's childhood, his grandfather, Arin, and the hopes of his father and the other revolutionary leaders in Baku, the entire mood of the novel alters. We can almost hear Koestler sighing with relief at the discovery that he is still capable of recognizing beauty, of admiring life. The story of Arin's marriage and the courtship of his daughter are compelling glimpses of human compassion. The dignity of Arin's simple politics, his belief in man's emergence from the monkey, is extended to the "high-ranking Commissar" whom they meet in Moscow; he "had the same quiet directness of speech and simplicity of manner as the men who had come to the room in Baku." These few, early chapters in the novel are Koestler's reprieve from a pulpit in Purgatory and provide the only lyricism in what otherwise may be called, using Julien's terms for a poem he cannot write, "the song . . . of the pox-ridden idealist."

Except for some subtlety in the comparison of Hydie's family and faith with Nikitin's, there is nothing here of Koestler's fascination for implicitness in metaphor or parable. Indeed, at points the narrative language is driven by a coarse violence that reflects the almost intolerable pressure of his conflicts with the French intellectual elite under which Koestler wrote the novel. Analogies between sexual and political perversions abound, chiefly because this language most readily expresses the contempt Koestler feels for the Left's delusions, but also because of his long-standing conviction that "the neurotic entanglements of the political instinct are as real, and no less profound, than those of the sexual instinct."[5] Vardi explains to Hydie: "We call demi-vierges a certain category of intellectuals who flirt with revolution and violence, while trying to remain chaste liberals." They are "voyeurs" of history, teasers of revolutionary power. All they do is "masturbate" with ideas and commitment.

*The Age of Longing* is Koestler's first attempt at sustained personal parody, and it is neither intellectually nor emotionally richer for it. He does not lack malice, but rather lacks the compelling energy of a comic imagination. Instead of a satiric vision driven to the limits of the grotesque or the pathetic, we are presented with easy ironies that are obviously important to Koestler's experience, yet cannot, like the best comedy, challenge the reader's own sense of individual and social values. In 1951 Koestler's readers would have had no difficulty identifying the objects of his satire. But this recognition has since become less immediate, and the portraits, which have little independence from their origins, have also become muted.

"Lord Edwards" is a Cold War *identikit* of Professors Bernal and Haldane, leading English scientists (the former, a crystallographer, the latter a geneticist) who spent a great deal of their time supporting the Soviet Revolution on committees and in print.[6] Julien explains to Hydie that "in his day Edwards was really quite a good physicist. . . . He joined the Movement thirty years ago, mainly because for an English aristocrat it was the naughtiest thing he could think of. Then gradually the witchcraft began to work on him." Since then Edwards has continued to revise his books about the nature of the universe to conform to the scientific trends endorsed by the Commonwealth Central Committee.

But as Edwards later admits to Leontiev, he has remained in the Movement really because it would be "positively indecent" to change allegiances after so many years, and besides "there is nothing else." Yet the portrait of Koestler's English "pervert" loses its satiric outlines because he devotes so much of the novel to shows that indeed there is nothing else of substance in this age of longing. And one of the few, admittedly minimal, consolations is that afforded by English decency. Edwards is the only one from the "Witches' Sabbath" to treat Leontiev's defection on a human level, and at the end he calls the welcoming attitude of the French poet Emile Navarin (Louis Aragon) to the impending invasion "treason."[7] But he is clearly redeemed by his Englishness, not by an actual change in his character. What began as a hostile parody of an individual becomes in the end an equally oversimplified, but more congenial, parody of national traits.

The treatment of the French intellectuals is more consistently malicious. Professor Pontieux is mainly a caricature of Jean-Paul Sartre, but also draws on Koestler's hostility to Maurice Merleau-Ponty who had attacked him at length for his conception of Rubashov in *Darkness at Noon*. Koestler found Sartre's famous existentialist principles almost as repugnant as his complex support for Russia. Pontieux, like Edwards, is well-meaning, but is more dangerously influential as the leader of "neo-nihilism." Koestler elaborates the specific tenets of this "piquant technique of intellectual masturbation" through a lawsuit against a pupil of Professor Pontieux for having poisoned expensive tropical fish with a double martini. His lawyer quotes Pontieux "to show that the 'why-notish' attitude in general served a high moral purpose and social function" and that emptying the martini into the aquarium had allowed the fish "to become free in the profoundest sense of the word."

Pontieux himself is a bumbling, essentially tolerant man whose ideas took on an unwarranted life of their own. "He is just a clever imbecile," Julien says. Although mentally incompetent, Pontieux is given credit for honesty. When the Commonwealth army occupies "the Rabbit Republic," he supports the refugees and is "duly branded by the Commonwealth press as a syphilitic spider." By insisting that Pontieux's intellectual influence is ridiculous, Koestler may be settling a personal grudge against Sartre, but at the cost of diminishing the novel's political force. His approach makes it impossible for us to feel a crucial danger in the philosopher's ideas or personality.

Koestler's sense of personal failure seems to have been greater with Simone de Beauvoir.[8] As a result, he reserves most of his undiluted malice for Madame Pontieux, and it is through her that he sharpens the debate between the leftist intellectuals and those who truly understand Europe's dilemma. She refuses to believe in the inevitability of an absolute choice between American aid and invasion by the Commonwealth. "But if choose one must I would a hundred times rather dance to the sound of a Balalaika than of a juke box." Her preference for the Commonwealth is political as well as musical. She declaims to an American cemetery analyst: "you are a negro-baiting, half-civilised nation ruled by bankers and gangs, whereas your opponents have abolished capitalism and have at least some ideas in their heads." Koestler does not ridicule her tirade. However blind she is, her views are tenacious, widespread, and must be taken seriously because they will determine the fate of a continent.

At points Koestler even conveys a sense of her genuine despair and desperate anger at the plight of France. But at the end of the novel he withdraws this perspective. Julien remarks about the arrest of Pontieux: "The funny side of it is that his wife has always been a real, honest-to-God Commonwealth agent." He has little doubt that she is one of "the rising stars of tomorrow." One can merely guess at Koestler's reasons for this drastic alteration in her character. Perhaps he felt he had given her too much humanity and thus had not clearly emphasized that her attitudes represented the intelligentsia's betrayal of France and the civilized world. The impending invasion seems to have worn away any need to distinguish between deliberate and unconscious forms of treason.

The only recognizable French intellectual who is both brilliant and patriotic is Georges de St. Hilaire, who "hates Pontieux and the neo-nihilists because he is probably the only true neo-nihilist alive." In sharp contrast with the rest of the caricatures, Koestler's sketch of his friend, André Malraux, is generous, warm, and admiring. Yet it also recognizes certain limitations.[9] Although he is already forming a resistance group, what drives St. Hilaire is a mixture of duty, nostalgia for the last resistance movement, and a conviction "that in the gesture alone, regardless of purpose, can the dignity of man find its ultimate fulfilment." Even he has not accepted the strict Cold War alternatives.

While he and Commanche are discussing the technical details of the underground, St. Hilaire also contemplates the memoirs he will write afterwards. Because his approach is clearly limited by its subjectivity, St. Hilaire is no political messiah. Nevertheless, his leadership represents one of the few possibilities for action in France. Through St. Hilaire, Koestler suggests that at a time when the lack of absolute faith is weakening an entire culture, even a belief in personal style, in gestures, can be politically significant. It can at least provide an impetus to endure until Julien's hope for "a cosmic loyalty with a doctrine acceptable to twentieth century man" becomes a reality.

The novel tries to establish an ongoing debate between Julien and Hydie about the nature of belief. Julien maintains that one should accept spiritual vacancy rather than be occupied by an inhumane, destructive faith. Under other, less desperate circumstances, Koestler suggests, Julien's argument would be indisputable, but with the bug of longing at an epidemic pitch, Hydie is closer to the truth when she insists that even a mirage is better than nothing, that the question of value is irrelevant to man's compulsive need to transcend himself. On these grounds, she expresses sympathetic admiration for the dignitaries at the rally and almost religious awe for Nikitin.

Throughout the novel Koestler demonstrates the inhumanity of Nikitin's doctrine as well as his personal insensitivity and cruelty. But these judgments are also a confirmation of his amoral strength. From the standpoint of a humanistic tradition, Nikitin is a repellent automaton, yet the present crisis results from the debasement and weakness of this tradition in the face of the strength in him and in the world he represents. Nikitin's analysis of the spiritual decadence in France is corroborated incessantly. The culture that gave the world "Descartes, Rousseau and St. Just" now spawns sterile philosophies like neo-nihilism and corrupt forms of Christianity. Its elegance, Commanche says, is now reserved for the art of dying. There is nothing elegant about Nikitin, but he alone is capable of disinterested loyalty and pure, if brutal, faith.

Hydie has a simple, though unfortunately phrased, credo: "If cafés were the home of those who had lost their country, bed was the sanctuary of those who had lost their faith."[10] The loss of faith means the loss of self-transcendence. A sexual relationship may allow the individual a temporary escape from the limitations of the self, but until she meets Nikitin, Hydie has not had even this fleeting gratification. Leaving the convent has not only bound Hydie to her body, but has also made her incapable of physical climax: "The nearer she knew herself to that elusive, ultimate fulfilment, for which her flesh longed as she had once longed for a sign of being chosen . . . the more bitterly disappointed she felt." Nikitin, however, has no such problems. The health of his "political libido" guarantees his sexual potency.

As she contemplates the beauty of her first Russian orgasm, Hydie realizes that the only other man she intuitively knew could bring her to fulfilment was her confessor at the convent. It is, of course, their faith "which made surrender to them an act of humility and devotion, free of guilt; which enabled them to lift her up, limp and willing, into their safe and fertile world where all doubts were dispelled." Because of "the impregnable fortress of his belief," Hydie submits to

Nikitin's insolence and condescension, until he shows
her how easily she can be returned to the solitariness of
the body and self. Then "humility" becomes humilia-
tion, and safety fear.

Koestler is suggesting that the Commonwealth will
overpower and humiliate its victims just as Nikitin has
dominated Hydie, although it is not likely to bring
Europe to new heights of physical pleasure. The affair
proves not only the intrinsic superiority and invincibil-
ity of ideological belief but also the supplanting of
Catholicism by Communism as a meaningful mass
faith. Whereas Hydie became disillusioned and left the
convent, as a boy Nikitin irrevocably "accepted a covenant more binding than any vow of a religious order."

Naturally, the novel abounds with religious allusions. Stalin is the "Antichrist," the Americans are planning a "Noah's Air Convoy," and everyone is awaiting
the Apocalypse. But this language has no special resonance since religious motivation is what Koestler sets
out to prove page by page. But there is a more compelling, if distasteful, pattern of imagery—that of physical
defects and disease. This language provides the only
metaphoric concreteness in what is, apart from Nikitin
himself, an abstract spiritual war fought with repetitive
arguments, inaction, and the most wearily intellectual-
ized sexual confrontation. It is a grotesque concreteness
that debases the characters and makes us aware of
Koestler writing not as a novelist, but as a scourge.
Through the parodies, through Hydie's weakness and
Nikitin's strength, Koestler indicts Europe for its lack of
values. But when he comes to describe characters,
moral indictment turns into immediate physical
punishment.

Hydie is generally attractive, but because her legs
are "heavy and rather shapeless," there is an incongruity
about her appearance that plagues her. Boris, one of
Julien's refugee friends, has tuberculosis and always

looks as though he is suffering from malaria. Julien himself is a composite of afflictions. He has a limp, a marked facial twitch, and a "wine-coloured burnt patch of skin" on one cheek. Through the course of the novel their appearance deteriorates. Boris appears increasingly cadaverous, Julien's limp becomes more pronounced, and Hydie's face grows "thin, with deep shadows under her eyes." Her submission to Nikitin has also caused her to develop a "nervous tic, rather like Julien's." All these flaws are symptoms of inner wounds, disharmony, and emptiness. Koestler victimizes his characters with a liberal distribution of assorted defects because it must be clear that they are unworthy of physical health.

The identification of physical and psychological states becomes more grotesque and dehumanizing as the novel progresses. Hydie's revulsion from the discolored nails and transparent skin of Monsieur Anatole's hand is related to her memory of her alcoholic mother's foul breath and the "pink pulp in her eyes." The representatives of the French bourgeoisie, whose "ancestors stormed the Bastille" and "gave the world the Rights of Man," are even more hideous. The wife has "huge breasts" and a "moist upper-lip." Her husband's chief interest is to examine "a fibre of meat" he removes from his mouth. The couple remind Julien of Circe's pigs; what has transformed them into beasts, however, is not magic, but the loss of any vital connection with their revolutionary ancestors, the commitment to nothing now except their mouths.

In fact, Koestler has always had a strange instinct for degrading characters through the texture of their mouths. During their debate about returning to the Commonwealth from exile, Julien notices that on Vardi's "thin lips the sweet vermouth had left an oily film which looked incongruous and repulsive." This image amply confirms that Vardi has made the wrong deci-

sion and also erases whatever human dignity he possessed. Julien realizes that Vardi wants an expression of
friendship from him, but this generosity is impossible,
not because of Julien's political rectitude, but because
he cannot "bear to look at Vardi any longer. A drop of
the sticky vermouth had trickled down from the corner
of his mouth to his chin; it looked somehow both obscene and frightening." Koestler's code seems simple,
even if harsher, than Nikitin's: without the moral harmony conferred by belief, man is nothing but a revolt-
ing parody of himself.

These images contrast sharply with the descriptions of the people in Nikitin's world. Whereas Monsieur Anatole's hand reflects the imminent death of the
civilization he extols, Nikitin's hand is strong: "It was
the large hand of a farm boy, with faint black rims
under the carefully manicured nails." Nikitin and his
family are morally dignified and physically attractive.
What diseases and physical defects they have are not
caused by psychological disturbance, but rather by
transitory social conditions. Arin received an injury during the Turkish persecution of the Armenians, but he
carries his stoop with great dignity, not shame. The
ugly pink mass in Hydie's mother's eyes is a symptom of
a more deeply rooted sickness than are the "sticky,
running eyes" of the children in Baku. All they require
are doctors, food, and cleanliness.

Both Hydie's conversion to Catholicism and her
eventual disillusionment are expressed in terms of disease and physical images. The "sagging figure on the
cross, the gangrened hands, the clawing fingers, the
crack in the drooping skull" initially suggested to her
the redemption of mankind through pity and love. But
confronted with a child suffering from cerebral menin-
gitis, Hydie decides that since nothing exists outside
God's will, He must be suffering "from some malignant
form of insanity." Nikitin's political faith can, however,
comprehend his father's malaria and the death of his

mother from puerperal fever. God is not a medieval madman, but a "great sterilising machine."

Julien is concerned with a different conception of madness. Underlying the "syphilitic," "sclerotic," "gangrenous" condition of Europe is probably a clinical insanity that results from a profound neurological flaw:

> Have you ever doubted that a hundred years hence they will discover that we have all been insane—not metaphorically, but in the literal, clinical sense? Has it never occurred to you that when poets talk about the madness of homo sapiens they are making not a poetical but a medical statement? It wouldn't be nature's first blunder either—think of the dinosaur. A neurologist told me the other day that in all probability the snag lies somewhere in the connections between the forebrain and the interbrain. To be precise, our species suffers from endemic schizophrenia. . . . Our misfitted brain leads us a dance on a permanent witches' sabbath. If you are an optimist, you are free to believe that some day some biological mutation will cure the race. But it seems infinitely more probable that we shall go the way of the dinosaur.

This diagnosis is one of the most important parts of *The Age of Longing*, at least in terms of understanding the remarkable continuity in Koestler's intellectual career.

Koestler initially began drawing together evidence of an evolutionary flaw in the structure of the brain in an early essay, "Anatomy of a Myth." Decades later, neurological schizophrenia became the central argument in the third part of his scientific trilogy, *The Ghost in the Machine* (1967). Because of an evolutionary mistake in the coordination of the old areas of the brain and the "new, specifically human areas," reason and awareness are at the mercy of the primitive instinct for self-transcendence. The earlier volumes, *The Sleepwalkers* and *The Act of Creation*, had shown that all human creativity is an expression of the self-transcending drive and the "older, underground layers" of the mind.

But Koestler concludes that this urge is "more

likely" to turn us "into killers" because it feeds on man's "immersion in the group mind."[11] When Koestler wrote *The Age of Longing*, whatever suspicions he had about the sources of rigid dogma were overcome by an even stronger feeling that the new god or spiritual creed he still hoped for was not yet forthcoming. Hence, he could see only the great need for something, anything, transcendental to revive the life instincts, if not the essential sanity, of a civilization. In *Twilight Bar* (1945), Koestler's least-known work and only piece of theater, he indulged the ideologue's ultimate fantasy—a confrontation between a morally pure extraterrestrial power and self-destructive mankind.

When the play opens, Glowworm is looking for material for his gossip column while the police are shooting "coolies" on Señora Gonzales's plantation. The radical leader and ex-barmaid, Bloody Mary, has broken out of jail and prophesies a "Massacre and Civil War," but instead two creatures, Alpha and Omega, appear, announcing that they have been sent to investigate earth's right to survive in the universe. Their own world needs more space for colonization, and they must liquidate the planet "on which life has the least meaning." At present earth is by far the unhappiest; its sickness is so profound it can actually be smelled across space. But if it can improve its Happiness Quotient in three days, it will be spared.

The prime minister and his cabinet debate "measures for the establishment of compulsory and complete happiness," but confronted with this challenge, easily agree to resign. Glowworm takes over, and thanks to a generous distribution of alcohol, the abolition of money, and the organizing skills of Señora Gonzales, there appears to be a substantial increase in happiness throughout the island. The movement has even started to spread. "Moscow has joined the New Era and started a purge against everybody who is unhappy." In the flush of his triumph Glowworm has a romantic interlude with one of the investigators who wants to return to earth after they have disinfected it.

Although everyone gathers to await the results of the investigation and pay tribute to "love, friendship and joy," there are rumors that the visitors are human, that a large amount of money has been found missing. On the strength of this, the "counterrevolution" begins. Coolies are being shot again, and the police, who are no longer called the "guardians of pleasure," have arrested the shimmering couple. Alpha and Omega refuse to tell Glowworm whether their "investigation" has been a hoax, and the play ends with an hour to go before the expiry of the three days allotted for man to choose salvation. Aside from the biographical interest it provides, *Twilight Bar* is noteworthy for its moral scheme and the continuity it too suggests between Koestler's literary work and the later, encyclopedic volumes on science and psychology.

One of the aliens explains that there is "an evil curvature" in space. There already may be a war going on between the "happy world" and the inhabited planets on the other side of the universe that worship pain and live "for the supreme aim of unhappiness." Earth is "particularly affected by the war," since it is on the border between the halves of the universe, "practically in cosmic no man's land." The difference between this fanciful vision and the faulty brain that causes man's endemic insanity is entirely one of vocabulary. The old and the new areas of the brain are in constant opposition, warring for the individual life and the history of the race. The possibility of reconciliation, of harmony, remains, but since man now possesses "power over life on the planet *as a whole*," his habitual self-destructiveness has grown closer to genosuicide.[12]

The first version of the play was written in Moscow in 1933 and served as a temporary escape from the many unconscious doubts and anxieties that had built up during Koestler's year in Russia. Koestler rewrote it in 1944, "during the last and for me most unbearable phase of the war," again as an "escape from the pressure of reality." The next war—for the spirit and the body of Europe—allowed Koestler no such relief. *The Age of Longing* is a bleak song of disease written in the meager hope that the truth he has seen will cure the blind, in the need at least to keep faith with himself.

# 7

# Doubts and Fatigue:
## *The Call-Girls*
## and Five Stories

After Koestler announced his "farewell to arms" and
need for a "vocational change" in 1955, he devoted his
considerable energy and encyclopedic imagination to
the history of science, to evolutionary theory, neurology, and extrasensory phenomena. In different ways
these often monumental explorations (*The Sleepwalkers*,
*The Act of Creation*, *The Ghost in the Machine*) all
concern the roots and manifestations of man's inherent
drive to transcend himself. But as a form of personal
transcendence, fiction was not entirely forgotten in
these decades. Koestler began to draft two novels, but
each was quickly abandoned.[1] *The Call-Girls* (1972)
finally emerged after the Alpbach Symposium that
Koestler organized in 1968 to counter the dominant
forms of scientific reductionism. Despite a similar loca-
tion and range of argument, the novel is not a strict
documentary rendering of the conference. It is instead
a survey of the ideas Koestler felt most compelled to
attack or defend in his methodical pursuit of the soul of
man.

Out of a sense of desperation for the plight of the
world (and some concern for the results of his own lab
tests), Niko Solovief, covert musician and a Nobel lau-
reate in physics, convenes a symposium, "Approaches
to Survival," and limits the participants to twelve, the
same number as the Apostles, who will, he hopes,

evolve a plan for the salvation of the species. What he has in mind is the letter that Einstein wrote to President Roosevelt in 1939, which initiated the nuclear era. "What the Einstein letter achieved might be called a miracle—a miracle in black magic. I wonder whether a miracle in white magic of a similar magnitude is beyond the reach of science." But he suspects that the plan is "harebrained." Eminent as they are, the academic call-girls have come for a modest honorarium and another chance to push their fragment of the truth.

As an account of a series of arguments, the novel has little physical or psychological action; no genuine process of change, or even the hint of change, occurs in the characters. When the symposium is not in session, however, there are glimpses of personal relationships, particularly the "mature" affections shared by Solovief and his wife, Claire. In her letters to *caro Guido*, who may or may not be her lover, Claire describes the "moth-eaten call-girls" and Niko's battered optimism. But more evocative is the understated worry for the fate of their son fighting in Southeast Asia. Throughout the novel the news of this war gets worse, and the threat of its escalation repeatedly punctuates the discussions.

In his opening address Solovief enumerates the chief reasons that the survival of mankind is "an unlikely possibility": the population explosion, nuclear proliferation, and, most lethal, "man's emotional immaturity compared to his technological achievements." Valenti, the neurosurgeon, concurs: "We are a horrible race, living in horrible times. Perhaps we should have the courage to think of horrible remedies." The promise of political effect arrives with Bruno Kaletski, a presidential adviser who hogs the debate and later weeps into his pillow out of shame. The promise of appropriate literary allusions and shock tactics is provided by Sir Evelyn Blood, the only poet alive, Solovief insists, with a knowledge of quantum physics. "Nobody *reads* mc," Blood proudly announces. "But every bugger in this country knows my *name*."

Despite the general tone of muffled weariness, Koestler does succeed in creating some passion in the way each "call-girl" holds his intellectual position. Horace Wyndham, who Solovief thinks will support the call for an action committee, focuses on the "battle of the womb," the "revolution in the cradle." By nourishing the brain even from before birth, the average level of human intelligence can be raised about twenty percent "within a single generation. This would be the equivalent of a biological mutation." The philosopher and sociologist, Professor Petitjacques, counters that man's tragedy is already an excess of intellect.[2]

Petitjacques's own position is a contemporary form of nihilism, an urban guerrilla warfare whose aim is "the disintegration of the entire social fabric, fibre by fibre," until nothing in the city is "safe for pedestrians sporting the conventional garbs of the system." The only "programme" is to have no programme. "No mirages. No illusions. . . . Just NO. *Nada, no, nix*, and down with the pigs, and *merde*." He was included in the symposium because of his influence with the new anarchistic generation—we should recall that the social context for the novel was the liberated 1960s—but Petitjacques elicits only contempt from the other participants as well as from the author and represents in the flesh the crisis they are attempting to address.

The major duel is between the anthropologist Otto von Halder (an ex-Nazi) and the zoologist Harriet Epsom (a liberal, but with certain physical and sexual problems). For Halder man is "a species of assassins— *homo homicidus* . . . a victim of endemic aggressiveness directed at his own kin." The only way to prevent "geno-suicide" is to ritualize man's aggression, to establish "outlets for violence on a mass scale" that would start in kindergarten and proceed through variations on the German dueling fraternities to "realistic war games" and Hate Sessions such as those pictured in Orwell's *Nineteen Eighty-Four*.

Harriet, who voices one part of Koestler's own position, insists that there is no "trace of evidence for a killer-instinct either in monkey or in man." Our "tragedy is not an excess of aggression, but an excess of devotion. ... It is loyalty and devotion which make the fanatic." By himself man is not a killer, but "the group is; and by identifying with it, the individual becomes one." History is not cluttered with personal vengeance, but with the consequences of "impersonal causes": Christian against Moslem, Protestant against Catholic. Harriet concludes by suggesting that if a "synthetic enzyme" could immunize man against this susceptibility, the battle for survival of the race could readily be won. Blood adds that language is a "heady poison" which only aggravates man's mass instincts.

After a decade of attacking behavioral psychology, Koestler could not refrain from including this heresy at the symposium table, if only as a foil against which more substantial theories can be measured. The rebuttal of behaviorism is effective, if coarse. Koestler has Blood quoting Koestler: "As my favourite writer said somewhere: the pundits of Burch's school have replaced the anthropomorphic view of the rat with a ratomorphic view of man." Professor Burch from Texas is genuinely puzzled by the fate of his children who had dutifully been raised according to his educational principles. Now one is a drug addict, and the other makes plaster casts of rock musicians' genitals.

Brother Tony Caspari's theory is somewhat less concrete. The Copertinian Order to which he belongs tries "to make use of all that science can offer to get a glimpse at levels of reality which transcend science." Like Koestler in *The Roots of Coincidence*, they are concerned with telepathy, levitation, and psychokinesis. For them contemplation is not "an end in itself," but "the most favourable condition" for tapping "the powers of mind at their source," which ultimately may change man's perspective on himself and his world. Solovief remarks that the "psi factor" seems more believable "in the light of the equally wild concepts of subatomic physics. . . . God is dead, but materialism is also dead, since matter has become a meaningless word."

But for Dr. Valenti causation has not been undermined by the current mysticism of physics. He expresses most of the neurological arguments Koestler had deployed in *The Ghost in the Machine*. Man's "instincts, passions and biological drives" originate in the "anachronistic" core of the brain that has "hardly been touched by the nimble fingers of evolution." In contrast, the modern neocortex has evolved at a tremendous rate, and as a result the structures have never been fully integrated. Thus, man suffers from an inherent mental disorder that leads him to "morbid infatuations" with impersonal causes.

But, Valenti argues, man is capable of repairing himself, of altering his "biological frontiers." When electrodes are implanted in the brain, individual patients can be cured of their primitive fear and hatred. Soon biochemical controls will be capable of modifying the hostility and aggression of mankind as a whole. The doubts and mistrust expressed by the other "apostles" at the conference are dramatically confirmed by the failure of Valenti's demonstration of "radio-controlled behavior" on his patient, Miss Carey. Because of "a minute fault" in his complicated wrist watch apparatus, she cannot control her hatred of the people disagreeing with her "saviour" and attacks Claire with a knitting needle.

Consequently, Solovief's summary of the proceedings is somewhat overshadowed by what appears to be the permanence and power of man's vestigial behavior. Undaunted, however, Solovief repeats the challenges facing the species that for the first time in history is burdened with the prospect of its complete extinction. In *The Ghost in the Machine*, Koestler had drawn the highly controversial conclusion that man must induce the necessary coordination between the old and new areas of the brain "by artificial means." Here Solovief announces that "we cannot wait for another hundred thousand years, hoping for a favourable mutation to remedy our ills. We must engineer that mutation ourselves, by biological methods which are already within our reach." Both fertility and "aggressivity-controls" have to be imposed on populations since, he argues, we do not "consult children before giving them vitamin pills."

Even Solovief's supporters cannot follow him to his logical conclusion of the arguments about the human condition, arguments they too were advancing. Wyndham "was saddened by Niko's frivolity—or the depth of his despair. Or both." The "call-girls" demur from his exhortation to form an action committee and "seek solutions on a planet-wide scale." Their only unanimity is to suggest having the proceedings of the symposium published immediately. But even this modest voice of reason and the neocortex is smothered by the primitive. Miss Carey sets fire to the tapes. Only cinders are left of the discussion, and what is left of Valenti's confident experiment are "some tiny bits and pieces of electronic equipment and dental cement." When Harriet says of Solovief that "he looks like the captain of a sinking ship," she is voicing an epitaph for all of Koestler's prophetic heroes and to some extent for Koestler himself.

When Koestler wrote *The Age of Longing*, neither his concern about the dangers of impersonal devotion nor his hardening perception of man's inherent insanity gave him pause to reflect upon his own impulse to condemn and brutalize the godless. But in *The Call-Girls* his role as prophet and scourge is also drawn into the welter of condemnation. Through the characters who articulate the arguments from *The Ghost in the Machine*, he seems determined to trivialize himself and for the first time in his published work wonders aloud about the purity of his mind and morality, about how much his voice draws its strength from the irrational nether regions of the ancient brain.

There is no doubt expressed about the fundamental accuracy of Harriet's argument that man is at his most dangerous when he commits himself to a set of ideas or a being larger than himself. But she is incapable of translating this understanding into appropriate public action. She is frightened of Solovief's radical solutions and remains bound not only to her "liberal, humanist" mind but also to her unattractive body. Her exotic miniskirt reveals "a pair of formidable thighs, made more fascinating by the blue veins wending their way through valleys of gooseflesh." Harriet's only answer to the issues raised by her own work and by the discussions at the conference is to seek out some Alpine sex, first with the bus driver, then with Helen Porter, a Kleinian psychologist with a shaved neck. For Koestler, sexual vulgarity is often an exact image of political weakness.

Valenti's weakness is more complex. Unlike Harriet, he is prepared to act upon his insights by treating individual aggression and working toward a "mental stabiliser" for mankind. But with his brittle good looks and space-arcade wrist watch, he is a menacing figure whose experiments are dangerous but awkwardly handled and whose equipment requires considerable improvement. How much, Koestler asks, could we trust a neurological antidote designed by someone so clinically suspect, someone who is furthermore a furtive

Catholic? Valenti is anxious to go to confession. "Father Vittorio loved to hear about the electrodes, and hoped to have one day Jesus needles implanted in all his flock." Like everyone else, Valenti is dominated by the ancient brain. Perhaps the exact diagnosis of man's insanity is merely a decoy action, another form of self-deception manipulated by our profound irrationality.

We must assume that with such doubts about the validity of his ideas, Koestler continued to insist upon the remedy of an imposed "mutation" because no better alternative was available and because it stood little chance of being adopted by the political powers. The moral certainty of the anti-Communist years had gone and with it his passionate, explosive hatred of specific people and certain kinds of attitudes. Even so despicable a call-girl as Professor Petitjacques could prompt only the most rehearsed gestures of disdain. The "fine spray" issuing from Petitjacques's lips is, of course, a mark of contempt, but the last picture is of the iniquitous sociologist, tucked up in bed, eating a box of chocolates, and reading *The Three Musketeers*.

The most eloquent emotion in the novel is a carefully hidden suggestion of Koestler's personal sadness. Solovief recalls that Claire used to call him a "melancholy hedonist." He asks: "Why not? Must one's obsession with the perils of mankind exclude the pleasure of being alive—of being still alive?" In his autobiography Koestler recalls with obvious pride that his political ally and difficult friend, George Orwell, had said: "The chink in K.'s armour is his hedonism."[3] Through Solovief Koestler is obliquely and nostalgically pointing to a period in his life that was full of literary and moral promise, when his pursuit of an ultimate vision was not tainted by suspicions of universal madness and delusion.

The only overt tension in *The Call-Girls* is created by the striking differences between the narrative of the symposium and the opening and closing sections, both of which were originally published by themselves.[4] The Prologue, "The Misunderstanding," is a thoroughly realized imaginative structure whose connection with the thematic center of the novel is immediate and powerful. Christ has chosen to die in order to awaken God who for some reason has withdrawn from his flawed world. "I could cure the sick and cast out a few devils, but that universal sickness of mind that has befallen your creation, that was your responsibility. And you did nothing about it. You were asleep. Once I even heard you snore through the sobs of a youth whom the soldiers put to torture."

But he is not entirely sure that God is indeed "asleep, or absentminded or otherwise engaged, and therefore unaware of the abominations and desolation of the world." If, instead, He is malevolent, or a "vapour of the desert, ignoble absence," or merely a "deaf and dumb spirit" immune to the suicide of a son, the cross will be both horrible and futile. Much of the force of Koestler's parable is this intense uncertainty felt by a thoroughly human Christ who takes pride in his hands and in his compassion. To make him more secular than divine, a rebellious, earthly Messiah, Koestler alters a number of details. Mary is "that tearful woman who keeps getting in my way." Peter is "that foolish fisherman of little faith," and all the apostles are "blockheads." Only the Governor grasped his plan. When he "turned his back and rinsed his hands," he was indicating "that this business could only be settled between you and me. So be it." Knowing that soon it will be too late to recant, to save his hands, he calls on his father to call off the charade, to become alive again.

The simplicity of style, the eternal battle between fathers and sons, the dim figures in the background only intensify the human pain and betrayal of this crucifixion. "This filth comes not out of me. This rising higher and higher up in white flames of pain happens not to

me. I am rising and sinking, turning on a wheel, riding in
the belly of the whale. The sun has turned black and
darkness fills the air." Koestler has frequently been
accused of having an inordinate and unhealthy skill
with the details of torture.[5] But there is no pleasure here
(artistic or religious) in the record of Christ's horror.
There is only sorrow that Christ's agony will echo
throughout time. Worse than feeling his body disinte-
grate is the understanding that in his name "they will
slay children for the love of a metaphor and burn
women alive in praise of an allegory." The will of the
father has prevailed.

In the novel Solovief wonders: "Where had he gone
off the rails? When he had let himself be carried away
by the idea of 'biological tampering'. If there was a road
to survival, it pointed in that direction. But did he really
believe in that 'if'?" This question of the perception or
the possession of insanity is extended to the concluding
fable, "The Chimeras," which is also about infection
and mutation. Anderson is trying to convince his psy-
chiatrist "that in a world which is being taken over by
the chimeras to be obsessed with chimeras is a healthy,
normal state of mind." But he does not want to remain
completely healthy and sane. "Life is unbearable when
you see clearly what's going on around you." Anderson
wants only a small "blind spot" so that the mutants—
obviously not those imagined by Koestler's earlier,
more optimistic heroes—will seem more like normal
people.

This parable about the burden of insight and the
blindness of the world is more cerebral and less reso-
nant than the Prologue, but has a kind of grim, postideo-
logical humor. As Anderson explains that one's "blind
spot expands" according to the grade of infection, Dr.
Grob's praise of therapeutic integration and societal
adjustment sounds increasingly leonine. Outside, "a
horde of chimeras was advancing . . . smashing windows and lamp-posts with their scaly tails, while their

goaty parts erupted in farts which turned into a poison-
ous, swirling cloud." Koestler is again the solitary voice
in the wilderness, describing the growing monstrosity
of the race. But for Dr. Grob, whether he is a flunkey for
the old brain, an existentialist philosopher, or an orthodox psychologist, the chimeras are just ordinary
"nice kids, full of vitality."

Koestler's fables of the crucifixion and the spread
of human madness also appear in his last collection,
*Kaleidoscope* (1981), with three other "Tales of the
Absurd." Like "The Chimeras," "Confrontations" details
a bizarre process of therapy. Tony has embarked on
what he calls an "experiment" of confession and conversation with Dr. Adamson because of dreams that
began while he was still working for the government.
The nightmare images are of an urgent telegram that he
is unable to decipher. "I know that I am bidden to make
a decision on a matter of life and death, but I can do
nothing about it." The text of the subsequent telegram
was clear, "but again I was unable to read it, because I
had broken my spectacles and the world had become a
blur." The guilt for his inability to act, to prevent the
"mounting" tide's invasion of "the dry land," becomes
more specific with each "experimental session" in the
company of Dr. Adamson.

Tony recounts that he had had "a good war," that
his job of collecting documentary evidence, particularly photographs, from the concentration camps had
not troubled him at all. Now, however, the most ordinary facets of life become grotesque creations of
empathy. Digging in the garden, he "suddenly understood . . . what it meant to be unable to stop digging
because there is a man behind you with a loaded gun."
He can easily imagine the physical relief and the sense
of pride of one who digs his own grave even as the
machine guns and tip-carts full of quicklime await the
completion of the job.

For Tony a newspaper used to light a log fire is also

an exercise in the unending drama of human suffering: "the paper rears up as if in savage pain, it writhes, shrivels, twists . . . like a human body burned at the stake." Taking pills to ease the agony in his mind will not stop the torture practiced by different regimes throughout the world. Even his resignation from his own government has done nothing to alter a policy he judges criminal. Because his Ministry considers it essential to safeguard access to "a certain rare mineral" controlled by "the Borovians," they are prepared to connive in the destruction of a smaller, less powerful tribe.

Dr. Adamson shouts at him that he should feel pride rather than guilt for this moral gesture, but that his attitudes are becoming increasingly obsessive and morbid, that he is a repressed sadist hungering for "ghosts of his own making." Frightened by the yelling, Tony's wife enters the study, but finds only one person there. Adamson has been his alter ego, "a shabby embodiment of logic and commonsense," providing Tony with the temptation to escape his guilt, his share in the world's agony, and at the same time a way of articulating and organizing his sense of absolute horror. All pain for him is eternally present. "The gas chambers are still working to full capacity, the witches chained to the stake still scream." When the tension between guilt and self-preservation becomes too great, he screams his hatred of himself, and the "therapy" ends.

Predictable as the ending is, and despite having no clear shape except as a pattern of accusation and defense, the story has a sharp, commanding power. There are no extravagant claims made for Tony's prophetic vision or intelligence. Although he forced himself to resign from his modest position, he kept "a discreet silence" about his reasons. All that distinguishes him from other people is that he has no immunity from the "virus . . . of guilt and anxiety" which saturates the air we all breathe. The language that Tony uses to deal with "Adamson" is straightforward and understated, but rises to meet the horrifying pitch of his misery in "the eternal now of unyielding despair." The lack of subtlety in the story is not a product of literary indifference, but rather of the need to emphasize with absolute clarity the burden of ordinary human responsibility.

"An Intimate Dialogue" concerns the boundary between the mind and the brain and is, therefore, more of an intellectual puzzle than a statement of moral compulsion, Initially, the mind asks his companion some undemanding questions about the age and origin of the universe, but problems of absolute meaning— "What was there *before* the Bang? Why is there something instead of nothing?"—only aggravate the brain and give it a headache. "On the authority of our most eminent logicians," brain says, these are meaningless questions, and besides, it has not been programmed to answer them. The mutual recriminations begin; brain ridicules the mind's belief in its immortality, and mind accuses its relation of blindness to metaphysical harmonies.

One twist in this dramatization of elementary philosophy is that neither wants to be tainted by association with God. "Anyway, the monster is dead. Rumour has it he was suffocated in one of those camps when the gas was turned on by his orders, or at least with his passive connivance." What divides them again, however, is the issue of ultimate creation. Mind insists that spirit, "the Word," produced flesh, whereas brain affirms the more material sequence, that an accidental collision of particles resulted in the world. In fact, mind itself was an "unintentional" by-product of haphazard chemistry.

Koestler succeeds very well in conveying a sense of the righteousness on both sides of what seems like a cosmic divorce action. Each is genuinely pained by the rigid delusions of the other. Moreover, their voices are distinctive. Mind is elegant, but condescending and smug in its aesthetic superiority; brain is aggrieved and almost vulnerable, but more malicious. If Koestler is at all partisan in the debate, it is in opposition to random, imprisoning materialism, but what troubles him more is their mutual detestation and the cycles of dominance they go through. The bases of all life, they wish for each other's death. Koestler wishes for their interdependence, their coordination, so that man can become truly human.

"The Control Tower" is the most thoroughly symbolic of the tales and in tone at least comes closest to the classical parables of moral and psychological mystery written by Franz Kafka. Uncertain about the date but not the inevitability of his execution, the speaker sees his prison as an airport sprawling "under its neon sky like a huge labyrinth whose exits and entrances no one knows." The officials are as confused as "the passengers or prisoners in their charge" who vanish without trace when they are called to the departure lounge. While they wait, the passengers distract themselves as they would outside the airport: by gardening, visiting museums and beauty parlors, and taking vitamin pills "to guarantee longevity."

Cut off from the Control Tower, the passengers are permitted to survey through the window of the Observation Tower a wondrous scene of comets, exploding suns, and "lazily circling" aged planets. Although they share a common fate, the passengers have split into hostile factions over this view. The larger group contends that all the phenomena are real; for members of the other faction it is "a cleverly contrived instrument of deception," an elaborate stage device. "In reality there is nothing outside the window and nothing inside the atom." To prove their own unreality and that of their opponents, they recently slaughtered a large group of Realists who were conveniently trapped in the illusion of matter.

Because of the inaccessibility of the Control Tower—directions to it are absolutely impenetrable—theories about its inhabitants and their laws "are another permanent source of conflict, and are propounded with murderous passion." One hypothesis is that having succeeded in creating the technologically advanced airport, the "dignitaries" allowed themselves to die from boredom. Another theory holds that the airport was once ruled by "benevolent sages" who were destroyed during "the Catastrophe," when lunatics from a spaceship attacked the Control Tower. One sage escaped and "is supposed to be still roaming the airport in various disguises, pretending to be a passport officer, barman or chiropodist," while distributing "subversive pamphlets" against the lunacy of the Control Tower. The speaker is critical of the rebel's spelling mistakes and the expressions of "fanatical hatred" that undermine the argument.

Despite the variety of theories about the Control Tower, there is general agreement that the rulers "are either mentally deranged or else that they are in fact computerised robots with a built-in engineering mistake." Just before his disappearance, a physicist described the origin of this derangement. The fundamental principles of physics are "the laws of symmetry and parity." There must be as many right gloves as left, the forces of creation must be equivalent to the forces of destruction, and "the total quantity of evil in the universe should not exceed the quantity of good." The real Catastrophe in the history of the airport was that first as a practical joke, then as addictive entertainment, the rulers upset "the universal parity between joy and pain." Now one shower room in Auschwitz overbalances all the airport's cathedrals and art treasures. Death and suffering increase, while the hints of human glory recede into the dimness of memory.

Many of the story's emphases are favorite Koestler themes: the murderousness of men in groups, the inherent factionalism that emerges under pressure, the hostility and distance of ultimate authority, the myth of a better time which has degenerated through malice or accident, and, above all, the flawed mind of the race. Artistically the story is uneven. As the symbol for a bureaucratic, technological world, an airport is perhaps too easy a choice, but it has at least the charm of accuracy.[6] Despite his years of theoretical devotion to fables and parables, Koestler did not fully master their imaginative demands. An allegorical form depends for its intellectual resonance on the involvement of the reader through a process of implication, a logical tightness of "event," and an almost translucent precision of symbols.

In terms of implication, Koestler's parables are generally effective, but here he includes and explains too much. The theories about the Control Tower are given an undue prominence over the lethargy, confusion, and haphazardness that should constrain every moment in the airport. But his success with the narrative voice almost redresses the balance. As in "Confrontations," it is the speaker's ordinariness that is compelling, but ordinariness shaped by resignation and incomprehension, rather than by guilt and sympathy. After all his years of exploring messianic instincts and visions, of dealing with the sharp edges of ideology, Koestler seems content in these tales to weave his narratives around a simple, even graceful, indignation at the unchanging weakness and cruelty of mankind.

# 8

## Conclusion

Despite the thematic jaggedness created by Koestler's fixed attitudes toward history and revolution, *The Gladiators* and *Darkness at Noon* may justifiably be included, together with Orwell's *Nineteen Eighty-Four*, Malraux's *Man's Fate*, and Solzhenitsyn's *The First Circle*, among the most significant political fiction of this century. No such claims can be made for his subsequent work. In the later novels a vigorous literary intelligence is still at work, shaping metaphor and structure, giving particular episodes a remarkable intensity, but it is stifled every time by Koestler's moral or personal impositions. As his philosophical isolation and messianic instinct deepened, he became increasingly reluctant to allow his fiction the detachment and independence he knew it required to be art rather than propaganda.

When he wrote his first novels, he still considered himself a socialist. Because his political isolation was not complete, he could through Spartacus and Rubashov dramatize the failures of the Communist Revolution, but without despair and without fully engaging himself in their conflicts. Soon, however, his belief in the possibility of a regenerated, independent Left seemed to be contradicted by events, and he developed the agreeable, if amorphous, idea of a new spiritual movement or moral energy emerging throughout Europe. Koestler refused to accept a place at the end of a phase in human history; he refused to be deprived of faith.

The decline in his fiction begins with *Arrival and Departure*, in which the personal need to articulate his prophetic vision flattens the novel's moral perspective and complexity of language. *Thieves in the Night* provides a reprieve from his messianic design, but here too personal feeling (his often uncontrollable hostility to "ghetto Jewishness") mars the otherwise compelling texture of the narrative. But in *The Age of Longing*, what indications remain of Koestler's commitment to imagination and form are mere gestures enfeebled by a profound theological frustration and personal defeat. Nowhere he looked in Western Europe was there any suggestion of vital belief, much less of a new god evolving through the ethical consciousness of men.

About this time Koestler relocated the terms of his vision from the social to the biological. Perhaps the pressure of the conflict between political absolutes would act as a "biological stimulus . . . which will release the new mutation of human consciousness."[1] Not only does this language reflect the transition from politics to science in Koestler's intellectual life, it also implicitly acknowledges that the moral change he foresaw, although still natural, was more difficult and internal than he had anticipated. A decade later the "mutation" he hoped for, indeed demanded, was still hidden in the folds of history, and he began to argue for an artificially induced "adaptive mutation," a biochemical corrective for man's unbalanced mind.[2]

This perspective, which is wearily repeated and heavily qualified in *The Call-Girls*, marks the complete fracturing of the new god Koestler had handed to Peter Slavek like a sacred vessel. But in the last years of his life, Koestler's concern with the inner secrets of the mind, with parapsychology, was augmented by a view of outer space. "It is nice to know that we are not alone, that we have company out there among the stars—so that if we vanish, it does not matter too much, and the cosmic drama will not be played out before an empty house."[3] This mellow comfort is echoed in the simplicity and restraint of Koestler's short fiction, his "Tales of the Absurd."

Although one regrets the encroachments of the prophetic on the integrity of the novels, there is something profoundly admirable, if terrifying, in Koestler's role as moral clinician and scourge. In a sense, after *Darkness at Noon*, Koestler's political art was not so much written as lived. A combatant for the salvation of Europe, he became his own "spiritual ferment," a "new global ferment" in himself. Awesome in an intellectually more traditional way is his vast work in the "life sciences." What permanent originality the trilogy has must be determined by another form of inquiry, but there is no question that Koestler has been thoroughly successful in making great issues of contemporary scientific theory accessible to the ordinary reader.

However far behind he left his literary imagination when he began to beat the ideological thickets of postwar Europe, Koestler's bond with history has remained secure. In France and Israel he left a definable imprint that is usually out of the reach of artists. He has made our choices more real and forces us to think, not just about the contortions of political morality, but about the scope of the intellect itself. For a generation of writers Koestler was the embodiment of "the god that failed," yet his influence has not been limited to the intellectual world. When I began writing this study, a barber who still hangs the portrait of Joseph Stalin on his wall expressed horror that Koestler should be accorded such respect. No doubt Koestler would have found this hatred more comforting than the measured judgments of literary history.

# Notes

# 1. The Koestler Life: An Arrow in the Twentieth Century

1.   The material in the introduction comes from Koestler's autobiography, *The Arrow in the Blue* (1952; reprint. London: Hutchinson, 1969) and *The Invisible Writing* (1954; reprint. London: Hutchinson, 1969), from conversations with him in 1969 and 1977 as well as from some reasonable guesses and deductions. Iain Hamilton's *Koestler* (London: Secker & Warburg, 1982) has been useful for chronological information, particularly about the postwar years. The texts of Koestler's autobiography, novels, and essays I have quoted in this study are in the Hutchinson Danube Edition except for the following: *Darkness at Noon* (London: Jonathan Cape, 1941), *Twilight Bar* (1945; reprint. New York: Macmillan, 1947), *The Age of Longing* (London: Collins, 1951), *The Trail of the Dinosaur & Other Essays* (London: Collins, 1955), *The Lotus and the Robot* (New York: Macmillan, 1961), *The Call-Girls* (London: Hutchinson, 1972), which has the Prologue and Epilogue.

2.   David Astor, "Crusader," *Encounter* LXI (July-August 1983): 33.

3.   See Sidney Hook, "Cold Warrior," *Encounter* LXI (July-August 1983): 12.

4.   George Mikes, "Arthur and Cynthia," *Observer Review* (7 August 1983): 21.

5.  Jabotinsky and the Revisionists were considered extreme by the official Zionist organizations. They were later seen as "Fascists" when an offshoot of the party became the terrorist group *Irgun Z'vai Leumi*. In 1943, when he arrived in Palestine, Menachem Begin took over the Irgun and reorganized it into a potent political force.

6.  Bernard Crick, "Koestler's Koestler," *Partisan Review* 2 (1982): 279.

7.  The interpretative value of Iain Hamilton's *Koestler* is perhaps best exemplified by this account of the Nadeshda experience: "After three weeks in Baku, where he had an unhappy love-affair, he crossed the Caspian Sea. . . ." (p. 23).

8.  See Hamilton, *Koestler*, p. 69.

9.  David Astor, "Crusader," pp. 31-32.

10. Michael Foot, "The Destroyer," *Encounter* LXI (September-October 1983): 58.

11. Hamilton, *Koestler*, p. 76.

12. Hamilton, *Koestler*, p. 104.

13. The original had been lost when Koestler escaped from France; he rewrote it in the summer of 1944 as an "escape" from the bleakness of the war.

14. Simone de Beauvoir, *Force of Circumstance*, trans. Richard Howard (Harmondsworth: Penguin, 1968), p. 118.

15. Clement Greenberg, "Koestler's New Novel," *Partisan Review* 13 (November-December 1946): 581.

16. Raymond Mortimer, "Arthur Koestler," *The Cornhill* 969 (1946): 219.

17. Hamilton, *Koestler*, p. 148.

18. Hyam Maccoby, "Jew," *Encounter* LXI (September-October 1983): 53.

19. Hamilton, *Koestler*, p. 161.

20. In Hamilton, *Koestler*, p. 169.

21. Sidney Hook, "Cold Warrior," p. 15.

22. Raymond Aron, "A Writer's Greatness," *Encounter* LXI (July-August 1983): 11.

23. David Pryce-Jones, "Chess Man," *Encounter* LXI (July-August 1983): 26.

24. Melvin J. Lasky, "Remembering," *Encounter* LXI (September-October 1983): LXI.

25. David Astor, "Crusader," p. 33.

26. John Beloff, "Psychologist," *Encounter* LXI (July-August 1983): 31.

27. Sir Peter Medawar, *The Art of the Soluble* (London: Methuen, 1967), p. 91.

28. George Mikes, "Arthur and Cynthia," *Observer Review* (7 August 1983): 21.

29. Stephen Toulmin, "The Book of Arthur," in *Arthur Koestler*, ed. Murray A. Sperber (Englewood Cliffs, N.J.: Prentice-Hall, 1977), p. 177.

30. Harold Harris, "Author," *Encounter* LXI (July-August 1983): 25.

31. Melvin J. Lasky, "Remembering," p. 64.

32. Maccoby, "Jew," p. 52.

# 2. Silhouettes of History:
*The Gladiators*

1. Koestler, *The Invisible Writing*, p. 478, p. 321.

2. Ibid., p. 323.

3. Ibid., p. 323.

4. George Orwell, "Arthur Koestler," *The Collected Essays, Journalism and Letters*, ed. Sonia Orwell and Ian Angus (London: Secker & Warburg, 1968), III, p. 237.

5. Koestler, *The Invisible Writing*, p. 325.

6. Koestler, *The Invisible Writing*, pp. 321, 322. This change of perspective mirrors a major development in the modern historical novel. The Marxist critic George Lukács maintains in *The Historical Novel*, trans. Hannah and Stanley Mitchell (London: Merlin, 1962), that despite both ideological and literary inadequacies, the considerable achievement of the German humanists, Lion Feuchtwanger and Alfred Döblin—both of whom were acknowledged influences on Koestler's method— was to reestablish the seriousness and public character of history, to conceive of the past in its moral and political dimensions. For too long novelists had used history merely as exotic decoration for their romantic and personal fantasies.

7. George Lukács, *The Historical Novel*, p. 271.

8. Peter Green, "Aspects of the Historical Novel," *Essays by Divers Hands* 31 (1962): 48.

9. Koestler, *The Invisible Writing*, p. 326.

10. Peter Green's phrase, "Aspects of the Historical Novel," p. 50.

11. Koestler, *The Invisible Writing*, p. 325.

12. For a discussion of language in historical fiction, see George Lukács, *The Historical Novel*, pp. 195-96. Because *The Gladiators* was originally written in German, one wonders whether its stylistic difficulties were to some extent the fault of the translation. But Koestler has insisted on its accuracy to the original.

13. Koestler, *The Invisible Writing*, p. 323.

14. Irving Howe, *Politics and the Novel* (New York: Meridian, 1957), p. 20.

15. George Lukács, *The Historical Novel*, p. 311.

16. Jenni Calder remarks that his approach "allows Koestler to suggest depth rather than analysis," that the true importance of Spartacus is his "place in history," *Chronicles of Conscience: A Study of George Orwell and Arthur Koestler* (London: Secker & Warburg, 1968), p. 146.

17. Koestler, *The Invisible Writing*, p. 437.

18. George Orwell, "Arthur Koestler," p. 238.

19. Jenni Calder, *Chronicles of Conscience*, p. 131.

# 3. The Mind on Trial: *Darkness at Noon*

1. Koestler, *The Invisible Writing*, p. 478.

2. Ibid., p. 479.

3. Stephen F. Cohen, *Bukharin and the Bolshevik Revolution* (New York: Vintage, 1975), p. xv.

4. Koestler, *The Invisible Writing*, p. 190.

5. Sidney Hook, "Cold Warrior," *Encounter* LXI (July-August 1983): 12.

6. George Orwell, "Arthur Koestler," p. 239.

7. Koestler, "*Darkness at Noon* and *The Strangled Cry*," *Drinkers of Infinity: Essays 1955-1967* (London: Hutchinson, 1968), p. 281.

8. Raymond Aron, "A Writer's Greatness," *Encounter* LXI (July-August 1983): 10.

9. Koestler, *The Invisible Writing*, p. 490.

10. Ibid., p. 491.

11. See David Caute, *Communism and the French Intellectuals* (London: Andre Deutsch, 1964), pp. 132, 186.

12. Maurice Merleau-Ponty, *Humanism and Terror*, trans. John O'Neill (Boston: Beacon, 1969), p. 2.

13. Koestler, *The Invisible Writing*, p. 492.

14. Ibid., pp. 479-80.

15. Alexander Solzhenitsyn, *The Gulag Archipelago*, trans. Thomas P. Whitney (New York: Harper & Row, 1974), I-II, pp. 409, 412, 414.

16. Stephen F. Cohen, *Bukharin and the Bolshevik Revolution*, pp. 375, 378.

17. Irving Howe, *Politics and the Novel*, p. 229.

18. Ibid., p. 229.

19.  Jenni Calder, *Chronicles of Conscience*, p. 129.

20.  John O'Neill, the translator of Merleau-Ponty's *Humanism and Terror*, remarks that Koestler does not know "how to grasp the lived relation between the senses and ideology in a man's character" (ix-x). Merleau-Ponty's argument is that in believing that "either conscience is everything or else it is nothing," Rubashov is following "a sort of sociological scientism rather than anything in Marx," pp. 14-15.

21.  Stephen F. Cohen, *Bukharin and the Bolshevik Revolution*, p. 240.

22.  Stephen Spender, "In Search of Penitence," in *Arthur Koestler*, ed. Murray A. Sperber, p. 104.

# 4. Therapy, Aesthetics, and the Divine: *Arrival and Departure*

1.  Koestler, "The Novelist's Temptations," *The Yogi and the Commissar and Other Essays* (London: Jonathan Cape, 1945), p. 34.

2.  Koestler, *Arrow in the Blue*, pp. 122-23.

3.  Philip Rahv comments: "Now a writer as thoroughly political as Koestler cannot but identify the nonpolitical life with a lower form of existence, that is to say, with the subhistorical," "Koestler and Homeless Radicalism," *Image and Idea* (Norfolk, Conn.: New Directions, 1957), p. 177.

4.  George Orwell, "Arthur Koestler," p. 243.

5.  Koestler, "The Fraternity of Pessimists," *The Yogi and the Commissar*, p. 100.

6.  Koestler, Postscript to the Danube Edition of *Arrival and*

*Departure* (London: Jonathan Cape, 1943), p. 190.

7. Koestler, *Arrow in the Blue*, p. 308.

8. Harold Rosenberg, "The Case of the Baffled Radical," *Partisan Review* (XI) (Winter 1944): 103.

9. Koestler, *Arrow in the Blue*, pp. 324-25.

10. Koestler, "The Yogi and the Commissar (II)," pp. 226-27.

11. Ibid., p. 224.

12. Koestler, *Arrow in the Blue*, p. 323, p. 303, p. 304.

13. V. S. Pritchett, "Koestler: A Guilty Figure," in *Arthur Koestler*, ed. Murray A. Sperber, p. 63.

14. Harold Rosenberg, "The Case of the Baffled Radical," p. 103; George Orwell, "Arthur Koestler," p. 242.

15. Interview with the author, 10 March 1969.

16. Koestler, *The Act of Creation* (London: Hutchinson, 1964), p. 337.

17. Koestler, *Beyond Reductionism* (London: Hutchinson, 1969), p. 230.

18. Koestler, "Artist on a Tightrope," *Drinkers of Infinity* (London: Hutchinson, 1968), p. 33.

19. "The Misunderstanding" and "The Chimeras" became the Prologue and Epilogue to *The Call-Girls*. See Chapter 7 for a discussion of them.

20. Koestler, *Bricks to Babel* (London: Hutchinson, 1980), p. 207.

21. Ibid., p. 212.

22. Koestler, "Artist on a Tightrope," *Drinkers of Infinity: Essays 1955-1967*, p. 38.

23. Koestler, "The Novelist's Temptations," *The Yogi and the Commissar*, p. 34.

24. Koestler, "The Yogi and the Commissar," p. 15.

25. Koestler, "The Novelist's Temptations," *The Yogi and the Commissar*, p. 39.

# 5. Old Means and a New End: *Thieves in the Night*

1. David Leitch, "Explosion at the King David Hotel," in *Age of Austerity: 1945-1951*, ed. Michael Sissons and Philip French (Harmondsworth: Penguin, 1964), p. 63.

2. Ibid., p. 73.

3. Koestler, Postscript to the Danube Edition of *Thieves in the Night*, p. 336.

4. Koestler, *The Invisible Writing,* pp. 463-64.

5. R. H. S. Crossman, "The Anatomy of Terrorism," *New Statesman* (2 November 1946): 321.

6. Koestler, Postscript to the Danube Edition of *Thieves in the Night*, p. 335.

7. Koestler, "The Challenge of Our Time," *The Trail of the Dinosaur & Other Essays*, pp. 13-14.

8. Ibid., p. 14.

9. Koestler, "The Fraternity of Pessimists," *The Yogi and the Commissar and Other Essays*, p. 105.

10. Ibid., p. 104.

11. Koestler, *Promise and Fulfilment* (London: Macmillan, 1949), p. 64.

12. Isaac Rosenfeld, "Palestinian Ice Age," in *Arthur Koestler*, ed. Murray A. Sperber, p. 51.

13. The phrase is V. S. Pritchett's "Koestler: A Guilty Figure," in *Arthur Koestler*, ed. Murray A. Sperber, p. 64.

14. In his essay Isaac Rosenfeld sees in Koestler "the peculiarly masochistic pleasure that many former Marxists now take in yielding to necessity—in their motivation there is present even an element of wickedness: the pleasure one takes in destroying others' illusions. . . ," in *Arthur Koestler*, ed. Murray A. Sperber, p. 51. Also see Maurice Merleau-Ponty, *Humanism and Terror*, p. xxxviii.

15. Koestler, *Arrow in the Blue*, p. 138.

16. Anthony Burgess, *Urgent Copy* (Harmondsworth: Penguin, 1973), p. 164; Edmund Wilson, "Arthur Koestler in Palestine," in *Arthur Koestler*, ed. Murray A. Sperber, p. 46.

17. Jenni Calder, *Chronicles of Conscience*, p. 215.

18. Koestler, *Arrow in the Blue*, p. 205.

19. Quoted by Iain Hamilton, *Koestler*, p. 135.

20. Clement Greenberg, "Koestler's New Novel," *Partisan Review* 13 (November-December 1946): 581.

21. Koestler, Postscript to the Danube Edition of *Thieves in the Night*, p. 335.

22.    Koestler, *Promise and Fulfilment*, p. 335.

# 6. The Pathology of Faith: *The Age of Longing* and *Twilight Bar*

1.    Koestler, Preface to the Danube Edition of *The Age of Longing*, p. ix.

2.    Ibid., p. x.

3.    Koestler, Epigraph to the original Collins edition, p. 8.

4.    Interview with the author, 10 March 1969.

5.    Koestler, "A Guide to Political Neuroses," *The Trail of the Dinosaur & Others Essays*, p. 216.

6.    Behind the caricature is a specific dispute as well, Koestler's heated public disagreement with Bernal's conception of a collective ethics, in "The Challenge of Our Time," *The Trail of the Dinosaur & Other Essays*, pp. 14-15.

7.    Louis Aragon, one of the founders of the Surrealist movement, was converted to the Communist Party for whose glory he wrote his novels and poems. Aragon also served in the Resistance during the war.

8.    Simone de Beauvoir: novelist, autobiographer, and for almost half a century, Sartre's companion. Her novels of the 1940s are concrete elaborations of existentialist conceptions of freedom and choice. *The Second Sex* is one of the modern world's most remarkable works about women. Her postwar novel *The Mandarins*

includes a thinly masked portrait of Koestler and the brief affair she had with him.

9. André Malraux: art collector, author of *Man's Fate* and *Voices of Silence*, traveler, creator of the Loyalist Air Force during the Spanish Civil War, and Minister of Culture under de Gaulle.

10. Jenni Calder contends that Hydie is simply motivated by boredom and "an irresponsible curiosity," *Chronicles of Conscience*, p. 220.

11. Koestler, *The Ghost in the Machine*, (London: Hutchinson, 1967) p. 245, p. 248.

12. Ibid., p. 322, p. 327.

# 7. Doubts And Fatigue: *The Call-Girls* and Five Stories

1. Iain Hamilton, *Koestler*, pp. 245, 291.

2. Petitjacques seems to be a parody of Herbert Marcuse, the revolutionary philosopher and "guru" of the American student movement in the 1960s.

3. Koestler, *The Invisible Writing*, p. 524.

4. "The Misunderstanding" originally appeared as "Episode" in *Encounter* (December 1968). "The Chimeras" was first published in *Playboy* (May 1969).

5. Notably by V. S. Pritchett, "Koestler: A Guilty Figure," in *Arthur Koestler*, ed. Murray A. Sperber, p. 63.

6.  There is some evidence that Koestler knew Rex Warner's *The Aerodrome* (1941), which uses the Air Force and its facilities as an allegory of fascism.

# 8. Conclusion

1.  Koestler, "An Outgrown Dilemma," *The Trail of the Dinosaur*, p. 194.

2.  Koestler, *The Ghost in the Machine*, p. 336.

3.  Koestler, "Cosmic Horizons," *Bricks to Babel*, p. 681.

# Bibliography
# Principal Works by
# Arthur Koestler

*Von Weissen Nächten und Roten Tagen* (White Nights and Red Days). Kharkov: Ukrainian State Publishers for National Minorities, 1934.

*L'espagne ensanglantée: Un livre noir sur l'espagne*. Paris: Editions du Carrefour, 1937.

*Spanish Testament* (including *Dialogue with Death*). London: Victor Gollancz, 1937.

*The Gladiators*, trans. Edith Simon. London: Jonathan Cape, 1939.*

*Darkness at Noon*, trans. Daphne Hardy. London: Jonathan Cape, 1941.*

*Scum of the Earth*. London: Jonathan Cape, 1941.*

*Dialogue with Death*, trans. Trevor and Phyllis Blewitt (Extracted from *Spanish Testament*). Harmondsworth: Penguin, 1942.*

*Arrival and Departure*. London: Jonathan Cape, 1943.*

*Twilight Bar: An Escapade in Four Acts*. London: Jonathan Cape, 1945.

*The Yogi and the Commissar and Other Essays*. London: Jonathan Cape, 1945.*

*Thieves in the Night: Chronicle of an Experiment*. London: Macmillan, 1946.*

*Insight and Outlook: An Inquiry into the Common Foundations of Science, Art, and Social Ethics*. London: Macmillan, 1949.

*Promise and Fulfilment: Palestine 1917-1949*. London: Macmillan, 1949.

With Others. *The God That Failed*. Edited by Richard Crossman. London: Hamish Hamilton, 1950.

*The Age of Longing*. London: Collins, 1951.*

*Arrow in the Blue: An Autobiography*. London: Collins with Hamish Hamilton, 1952.*

*The Invisible Writing: An Autobiography.* London: Collins with Hamish Hamilton, 1954.*

*The Trail of the Dinosaur & Other Essays.* London: Collins, 1955.*

*Reflections on Hanging.* London: Victor Gollancz, 1956.*

*The Sleepwalkers: A History of Man's Changing Vision of the Universe.* London: Hutchinson, 1959.*

With C. H. Rolph. *Hanged by the Neck: An Exposure of Capital Punishment in England.* Harmondsworth: Penguin, 1961.

*The Lotus and the Robot.* London: Hutchinson, 1961.*

Editor. *Suicide of a Nation? An Enquiry into the State of Britain Today.* London: Hutchinson, 1963.

*The Act of Creation.* London: Hutchinson, 1964.*

*The Gho st in the Machine.* London: Hutchinson, 1967.

*Drinkers of Infinity: Essays 1955-1967.* London: Hutchinson, 1968.

Editor, with J. R. Smythies. *Beyond Reductionism: New Perspectives in the Life Sciences: The Alpbach Symposium.* London: Hutchinson, 1969.

*The Case of the Midwife Toad.* London: Hutchinson, 1971.

*The Call-Girls.* London: Hutchinson, 1972.*

*The Roots of Coincidence.* London: Hutchinson, 1972.

With Sir Alister Hardy and Robert Harvie. *The Challenge of Chance.* London: Hutchinson, 1973.

*The Heel of Achilles: Essays 1968-1973.* London: Hutchinson, 1974.

With Arnold Toynbee and Others. *Life after Death.* London: Weidenfeld & Nicolson, 1976.

*The Thirteenth Tribe: The Khazar Empire and Its Heritage.* London: Hutchinson, 1976.

*Janus: A Summing Up.* London: Hutchinson, 1978.

*Bricks to Babel: Selected Writings with Comments by the Author.* London: Hutchinson, 1980.

*Kaleidoscope.* London: Hutchinson, 1981.*

*Note: An asterisk denotes a volume issued by Hutchinson in the uniform Danube Edition.

# Selected Books and Articles on Arthur Koestler

Atkins, John. *Arthur Koestler.* London: Neville Spearman, 1956.

Axthelm, Peter M. *The Modern Confessional Novel.* New Haven: Yale University Press, 1967.

Beauvoir, Simone de. *Force of Circumstance.* Translated by Richard Howard. Harmondsworth: Penguin, 1968.

———. *The Mandarins.* Translated by Leonard M. Friedman. London: Fontana, 1960.

Benson, Frederick R. *Writers in Arms.* New York: New York University Press, 1967.

Beum, Robert. "Epigraphs for Rubashov: Koestler's *Darkness at Noon.*" *Dalhousie Review* 42 (Spring 1962): 86-91.

Burgess, Anthony. "Koestler's Danube." in *Urgent Copy: Literary Studies* London: Jonathan Cape, 1968.

———. *The Novel Now.* London: Faber, 1967.

Calder, Jenni. *Chronicles of Conscience: A Study of George Orwell and Arthur Koestler.* London: Secker & Warburg, 1968.

Caute, David. *Communism and the French Intellectuals 1914-1960.* London: André Deutsch, 1964.

Chiaromonte, Nicola. "Koestler or Tragedy Made Futile." *Politics* (September 1945): 266-70.

Cohen, Stephen F. *Bukharin and the Bolshevik Revolution: A Political Biography 1888-1938.* New York: Alfred A. Knopf, 1973.

Conquest, Robert. *The Great Terror: Stalin's Purge of the Thirties.* Rev. ed. Harmondsworth: Penguin, 1971.

Crick, Bernard. "Koestler's Koestler." *Partisan Review* 2 (1982): 274-83.

Crossman, R. H. S. "The Anatomy of Terrorism" [Review of *Thieves in the Night*]. *New Statesman* (2 November 1946): 321-22.

———."Darkness at Night" [Review of *The Age of Longing*]. *New Statesman* (28 April 1951): 482-84.

Davis, Robert Gorham. "The Sharp Horns of Koestler's Dilemmas." *The Antioch Review* 4 (Winter 1944-45): 503-17.

Debray-Ritzen, Pierre, ed. *Arthur Koestler*. Paris: Editions de l'Herne, 1975.

Deutscher, Isaac. *Heretics and Renegades*. London: Jonathan Cape, 1955.

Drucker, H. M. *The Political Uses of Ideology*. London: Macmillan, 1974.

Fiedler, Leslie. "Toward the Freudian Pill" [Review of *The Ghost in the Machine*]. *New Statesman* (27 October 1967), 548-49. Reprinted in *Arthur Koestler: A Collection of Critical Essays*. Edited by Murray A. Sperber. Englewood Cliffs, N.J.: Prentice-Hall, 1977.

Garaudy, Roger. "The Lie in Its Pure State: Arthur Koestler." In *Literature of the Graveyard*. New York: International Publishers, 1948.

Grossman, Edward. "Koestler's Jewish Problem." *Commentary* 62 (December 1976): 59-64.

Hamilton, Iain. *Koestler: A Biography*. London: Secker & Warburg, 1982.

Harris, Harold, ed. *Astride the Two Cultures: Arthur Koestler at 70*. London: Hutchinson, 1975.

Hicks, Granville. "Arthur Koestler and the Future of the Left." *The Antioch Review* 5 (Summer 1945): 212-23.

Hoffman, Frederick J. "*Darkness at Noon*: The Consequences of Secular Grace." *The Georgia Review* 13 (Fall 1959): 331-45.

Howe, Irving. *Politics and the Novel*. New York: Meridian, 1957.

Huber, Peter Alfred. *Arthur Koestler: Das literarische Werk*. Zurich: Fretz & Wasmuth, 1962.

Klingopulos, G. D. "Arthur Koestler." *Scrutiny* 16 (June 1949): 82-92.

Levene, Mark. "Arthur Koestler: On Messiahs and Mutations." *Modernist Studies* 2 (1977): 37-48.

Lewis, John, and Reginald Bishop. *The Philosophy of Betrayal*. London: The Russia Today Society, 1945.

Mays, Wolfe. *Koestler*. Guilford: Lutterworth, 1973.

Medawar, Peter. *The Art of the Soluble*. London: Methuen, 1967.

Merleau-Ponty, Maurice. *Humanism and Terror*. Translated by John O'Neill. Boston: Beacon, 1969.

Mortimer, Raymond. "Arthur Koestler." *The Cornhill Magazine* 969 (Winter 1946): 213-22.

Mudrick, Marvin. "Wooldridge, Koestler, and Watson: Prometheus at Work and Play." In *On Culture and Literature*. New York: Horizon, 1970.

Nedava, J. *Arthur Koestler: A Study*. London: Robert Anscombe, 1948.

Nott, Kathleen. "Koestler and His Critics." *Encounter* 30 (February 1968): 76-81.

Orwell, George. "Arthur Koestler." In *The Collected Essays, Journalism and Letters*. Edited by Sonia Orwell and Ian Angus. Vol. III. London: Secker & Warburg, 1968.

Pearson, Sidney A., Jr. *Arthur Koestler*. Boston: Twayne, 1978.

Pritchett, V. S. "Arthur Koestler." *Horizon* 15 (May 1947): 233-47. Reprinted as "Arthur Koestler: A Guilty Figure" in *Arthur Koestler: A Collection of Critical Essays*. Edited by Murray A. Sperber. Englewood Cliffs, N.J.: Prentice-Hall, 1977.

Rahv, Philip. "Koestler and Homeless Radicalism." In *Image and Idea*. Rev. ed. Norfolk, Conn.: New Directions, 1957.

Redman, Ben Ray. "Arthur Koestler: Radical's Progress." *College English* 13 (December 1951): 131-36.

Rosenberg, Harold. "The Case of the Baffled Radical." *Partisan Review* 11 (Winter 1944): 100-03. Reprinted in *Arthur Koestler: A Collection of Critical Essays*. Edited by Murray A. Sperber. Englewood Cliffs, N.J.: Prentice-Hall, 1977.

Rosenfeld, Isaac. "Palestinian Ice Age." *The New Republic* 115 (4 November 1946): 592-93. Reprinted in *Arthur Koestler: A Collection of Critical Essays*. Edited by Murray A. Sperber. Englewood Cliffs, N.J.: Prentice-Hall, 1977.

Rühle, Jürgen. *Literature and Revolution*. Translated and

edited by Jean Steinberg. New York: Praeger, 1969.

Siegel, Paul N. *Revolution and the 20th-Century Novel*. New York: Monad Press, 1979.

Solzhenitsyn, Alexander. *The Gulag Archipelago I-II*. Translated by Thomas P. Whitney. New York: Harper & Row, 1974.

Spender, Stephen. "In Search of Penitence." In *Arthur Koestler: A Collection of Critical Essays*. Edited by Murray A. Sperber. Englewood Cliffs, N.J.: Prentice-Hall, 1977.

Sperber, Murray A., ed. *Arthur Koestler: A Collection of Critical Essays*. Englewood Cliffs, N.J.: Prentice-Hall, 1977.

Strachey, John. *The Strangled Cry, and other unparliamentary papers*. London: Bodley Head, 1962.

Swingewood, Alan. "The Revolution Betrayed: Koestler and Serge." In *The Novel and Revolution*. London: Macmillan, 1975.

Toulmin, Stephen. "The Book of Arthur" [Review of *The Ghost in the Machine*]. *The New York Review of Books* (11 April 1968), pp. 16-21. Reprinted in *Arthur Koestler: A Collection of Critical Essays*. Edited by Murray A. Sperber. Englewood Cliffs, N.J.: Prentice-Hall, 1977.

Weintraub, Stanley. *The Last Great Cause: The Intellectuals and the Spanish Civil War*. New York: Weybright and Talley, 1968.

Wilding, Michael. *Political Fictions*. London: Routledge & Kegan Paul, 1980.

Woodcock, George. "Arthur Koestler." In *The Writer and Politics*. London: The Porcupine Press, 1948.

# Tributes and Appraisals

Mikes, George. "To Hell with Moderation." *Observer Review* (31 July 1983): 21.

Mikes, George. "Arthur and Cynthia." *Observer Review* (7 August 1983): 21.

"The Life & Death of Arthur Koestler." Contributions by Raymond Aron, Sidney Hook, Harold Harris, and others. *Encounter* LXI (July-August 1983): 9-37.

"The Life & Death of Arthur Koestler (II)." Contributions by John Wain, Hyam Maccoby, Brian Inglis, and Melvin J. Lasky. *Encounter* LXI (September-October 1983): 45-64.

# Index